Peace Soldiers

Peace Soldiers

The Sociology of a United Nations Military Force

The University of
Chicago Press
Chicago and London

Charles C. Moskos, Jr.

CHARLES C. MOSKOS, Jr., is chairman
of the Department of Sociology at
Northwestern University. He is the author
of *The Sociology of Political Independence*
and *The American Enlisted Man*, and is the
editor of *Public Opinion and the Military
Establishment.*

The University of Chicago Press, Chicago 60637
The University of Chicago Press, Ltd., London

© 1976 by The University of Chicago
All rights reserved. Published 1976
Printed in the United States of America

Library of Congress Cataloging in Publication Data

Moskos, Charles C
  Peace soldiers.

  Includes index.
  1. United Nations—Armed Forces. I. Title.
JX1981.P7M68   301.5'93   75-5070
ISBN 0-226-54225-4

PAIS

For Ilca

Contents

Tables

Acknowledgments

There ought to be a maxim in sociological field research: Those who should help you won't; those who can help you might. When I began this study of peacekeeping forces, I first went to the United Nations Organization in New York City to seek guidance, only to be received with bureaucratic curtness. Thus, when I later arrived in Cyprus, I had neither advance introductions nor any personal claim whatsoever to expect cooperation. But to my everlasting gratitude, once I presented myself to the United Nations Force in Cyprus or UNFICYP (pronounced OON-feh-sip), I was given virtual carte blanche to carry out the investigations which make up the core of this book. Indeed, the reaction UNFICYP accorded the probings of a sometimes too persistent guest was nearly always one of openness and, most often, good fellowship as well. And, it is to be openly acknowledged, my reception was made easier because I have spent most of my professional life studying soldiers, a group of men whose company I have always treasured.

Two people in particular helped the whole endeavor come out successfully. Major Søren Wissum of the Danish army, who knows more about UNFICYP than any other person ever will, became my research confidant. Whenever I was confused, Søren Wissum brought me clarity. And the practical matter of arranging all manner of entrees and field visits throughout UNFICYP was made possible only through the innovative efforts of my friend Svend Frandsen, then of the UNFICYP Military Information Office.

I wish to extend a special note of appreciation to two medical doctors in the Austrian Field Hospital who volunteered so much of their time and considerable talents to cure my wife of a serious ailment. Thank you, Doctors Fritz Bohmann and Franz Lackner.

During and after my stay with UNFICYP so many officers and men were directly helpful to this study that it is difficult to mention more than a few. Those whose help I especially relied upon were: Otto Tiefenbrunner of Austria; C. A. U. "Sandy" Cotton, Orville Lester, R. L. McKee, and Daniel Ryan of Canada; Erik Houkjaer and C. H. Christensen of Denmark; Jouko Erakare and R. K. Raitasaari of Finland; Stanley Crawford, Randall Cross, and Jack Fiskel of Great Britain; Kiernan Bradley, Joseph Cousins, and Kevin Duffy of Ireland; and Erik Bonde and Lief Hallberg of Sweden.

Throughout the preparation and conceptualization of this study I have argued with and learned much from Morris Janowitz. His own landmark work on armed forces and society continues to be a model for my own efforts. Chadwick F. Alger constructively criticized portions of the manuscript. Mrs. Elizabeth Conner, who has always been able to meet my impossibly short deadlines, typed the manuscript in her own inimitable manner of good humor and dispatch.

My extended stay in Cyprus was made possible by a 1969–70 Ford Foundation Faculty Fellowship, and I received additional research funds from the Council for Intersocietal Studies and the Research Committee of Northwestern University. This book took written shape while I was visiting at the University of Texas, and I wish to acknowledge the generous and stimulating atmosphere of the distinguished sociology department at that university. The final completion of this study and its expansion into a full-length monograph were made feasible only by a grant from the Army Research Institute for the Behavioral and Social Sciences. I am especially grateful to the good offices of Dr. David R. Segal. It must be stressed, however, that the usual caveat of the author alone accepting responsibility for the interpretations and conclusions is especially relevant in this study.

While in Cyprus I naturally also spent much time outside the UNFICYP orbit. My wife and I were pleased to make friends with many of the fine people of Cyprus—on both the Greek and Turkish sides. Our fond thoughts of what became almost familial ties are saddened because many of our Cypriot friends are now homeless—and may never go home again. That peace has always been a tenuous proposition on that island—and in far too many other places—is the best argument for this academic effort to clarify and further our knowledge of the military sociology of peacekeeping.

January 1975
Evanston, Illinois

Military Peacekeepers: Concepts and Characterizations

"Peace Soldiers"—the very term seems contradictory. But it does imply a model of armed forces which is compatible with the genuinely novel imperatives of the peacekeeping role as well as with many conventional aspects of military organization. The task before us is to understand the social factors that favor or hinder the peacekeeping role among the *actual* soldiers of a United Nations military force. This is also to say that the reader will not find a discussion of the conditions leading to the outbreak or cessation of hostilities between or within nations. Neither is this an account of the political, legal, or financial circumstances involved in the establishment of international peacekeeping forces. The literature on these topics is already quite impressive.

Rather, this is a study and research report in military sociology which seeks to specify issues having general applicability to armed forces charged with peacekeeping responsibilities. What are the organizational features of the military system which impinge upon the peacekeeping assignment? How do traditional notions of soldierly honor accommodate to the requirements of the peacekeeping role? Does service in an international military force require or diminish more parochial loyalties? Is military professionalism consistent or incompatible with the peacekeeping task? To answer these and related questions this study must be both narrower and broader than previous writings on the subject. It is more constrained in that its focus is almost entirely on the military dimension of peacekeeping. It is more inclusive in that it seeks to generalize from the materials of one body of peacekeeping soldiers to more general issues of attitude formation and institution building which bear on the central issue of the efficacy of armed forces for peacekeeping missions.

Definitions of a peacekeeping force are almost as numerous as commentators on the subject. From among various accounts, however, we distinguish two elemental themes underlying the pure type formulation of a peacekeeping force: *noncoercion* and *impartiality*. Although trying to deduce what is a bona fide peacekeeping force from such abstract principles may be futile, it is germane to mention some of the conceptual questions inherent in such an attempt.

Noncoercion has been described over a continuum ranging from Gandhi-like pacifism through self-defense to strictly limited applications of force as a last resort. But as it approaches the last situation—with varied interpretations of what determines a last resort—the concept of noncoercion loses meaning. Yet in the mandates of all extant and previous peacekeeping forces, the strictures on the use of force have been anchored to the standard of noncoercion—always allowing, however, for self-defense. In the actual field situation, moreover, the principle of self-defense can shade over into the minimal application of force and on rare occasions even give way to authorization for armed forces to accomplish local objectives. The shifting criteria of what constitutes self-defense thus become a central concern in any analysis of peacekeeping soldiers. For now it is enough to say that the notions of either noncoercion or self-defense in the peacekeeping context remain more of an ideal standard than an absolute guide for field operations.

In contrast to that peace theory which proceeds from the premise of noncoercion and then conceptually seeks to structure a peacekeeping operation meeting this desideratum, the military sociologist is more prone to accept the principle of the use of armed force and then conceptually examine how force can be regulated, diminished, and possibly eliminated in the peacekeeping task. To the degree that a peacekeeping force deemphasizes the application of violence in order to attain viable political compromises, such a peacekeeping force approaches the constabulary model of military forces proposed by Morris Janowitz.[1] The constabulary model recognizes that the use or threat of force must be carefully adjusted to the political objectives pursued. In the peacekeeping situation this could well entail—and often has—something approaching noncoercion. Rather than being concerned only with efficient achievement of victory, without regard to nonmilitary considerations, the peacekeeper is charged with maintaining the peace even to the detriment of military considerations. Although the constabulary model as originally formulated does allow for measured, if minimal, force in extremis to attain political goals, the military peacekeeper, in theory at least, resorts to force only in self-defense. Thus the peace soldier is an extreme ramification of the constabulary model. And this most stringent conception of the constabulary ethic—absolute minimal force—is the referent for this study of United Nations peacekeeping soldiers.

Even though initially proposed in the context of military professionalism devoted to national goals, the constabulary model easily encompasses multinational forces charged with impartial peacekeeping missions. Impartiality means that the peacekeeping soldiers have no apparent interest in seeing the moral vindication or material triumph of either of the disputants. Of course impartial intent can inadvertently further the cause of one of the disputants. Thus, in the most preferred circumstance impartiality means that the disputants themselves and other concerned parties consent to the presence and activities of the peacekeeping force. Such impartiality, moreover, seems most maximal if such forces have an international composition. Although under certain conditions regional peacekeeping forces can meet these criteria, in the contemporary world such forces are ideally authorized by and representative of the United Nations.

Because peacekeeping forces are recruited from units and personnel of preexisting national armies, the paramount question is whether the imperatives of noncoercion and impartiality require a reformulation of conventional military socialization and a restructuring of standard military organization. Certainly the constabulary ethic with its precepts of reliance on absolute minimum force runs against the customary grain of military behavior. Impartiality, when manifest in the mission of a world body, also implies that the traditional subjection of the soldier to the nation-state must be superseded during the period of peace-keeping service to a broader international loyalty. Yet the canons of military professionalism have rarely been examined in precisely these terms—an empirical deficiency which this study hopes to remedy.

With due cognizance of the ambiguity and complexity of the above considerations, we can, nevertheless, offer the following as a working definition of a *peacekeeping force*: military compo-nents from various nations, operating under the command of an impartial world body and committed to the absolute minimum use of force, which seek to reduce or prevent armed hostilities. The more generic term *peacekeeping operations* includes not only peacekeeping military forces but also such diverse and usually smaller peacekeeping enterprises as observer groups, truce com-missions, investigatory missions, and the like. The *peace soldier* is, therefore, one who serves in a military capacity under a command authorized by an internationally accepted mandate and who adheres to impartiality while subscribing to the strictest standards of absolute minimal force functionally related to self-defense. A review of the extant research on military peacekeepers will set the backdrop for a direct examination of the serving soldiers of an actual United Nations force.

Social Research on Military Peacekeepers

Between 1956 and 1974 an estimated 250,000 to 300,000 soldiers served under the UN flag. Surprisingly enough, the United Nations itself has conducted hardly any research on the functioning of peacekeeping forces. In 1965, the General Assembly did establish a Special Committee on Peacekeeping Operations, made up of thirty-three members and suitably balanced geographically and politically. But almost a decade later this committee, after several metamorphoses, had yet to authorize, much less complete, any studies of peacekeeping forces. Even the United Nations Institute for Training and Research (UNITAR)—a semiautono-mous UN body financed by governmental and private funds—has so far scrupulously avoided the incorporation of peacekeeping forces in its purview. UNITAR has confined its activities to seminars for civilian officials assigned to UN nonmilitary missions and the preparation of manuals for UN technical assistance.[2]

A different bureaucratic history but the same limited research output marks the experiences of the office of the Military Adviser to the Secretary-General. This office was originally established in 1956 by Dag Hammerskjöld to obtain practical guidance on military organizational matters confronting the United Nations peacekeeping force in the Middle East. Strictly advisory, the new office worked closely with Ralph Bunche, who as undersecretary for political affairs played a central role in overall supervision of peacekeeping operations throughout much of the 1950s and 1960s. With the advent of the United Nations force in the Congo, Hammarskjöld reestablished the post of Military Adviser in 1960 by the appointment of Indian Major General Indar Jit Rikhye. Despite the Secretariat's needs, the Military Adviser's office never consisted of more than four persons, and by 1969 the senior position of military adviser was abolished. Since that time the office has declined in both staff and relevance. Handicapped by its small size and constant attention to day-to-day peacekeeping details, the Military Adviser's office never had the time to engage in serious research on peacekeeping forces. Nevertheless, the office's staff did help design standby peacekeeping programs for contributing nations and put into writing some guidelines and handbooks on peacekeeping requirements in the field. Regrettably, these materials have never been publicly released, although a partial codification of the military side of peacekeeping operations can be found in the unofficial articles of General Rikhye.[3]

The bulk of evaluation and research on peacekeeping operations has been undertaken by parties outside the formal framework of the United Nations. In February 1964, the Norwegian Institute of International Affairs sponsored an international conference in Oslo to discuss "UN Security Forces as a Means to Promoting Peace." The participants included military officers with peacekeeping experience, administrators in international security operations, and concerned scholars. The Oslo meeting was followed in November 1964 by a conference in Ottawa sponsored by the Canadian government and attended by representatives of twenty-three governments that had earmarked forces for UN peacekeeping operations or had made significant contributions to them. In November 1965, the Norwegian Institute of International Affairs sponsored a second Oslo conference with the purpose of exchanging information among the principal earmarking nations. Additionally, the Canadian government and several of the Scandanavian governments had prepared various statements on the organization and training of their peacekeeping forces. These papers were informally circulated to other member governments of the United Nations.

There have also been efforts to institutionalize peacekeeping research and information exchange on a private, nongovernmental basis. In 1966, the World Veterans Federation established the International Center on Peace-Keeping Operations (IPKO). Owing to insufficient financial backing, IPKO lasted only two years. During its short existence it did initiate an information channel which distributed a variety of hitherto elusive documents —many translated into English for the first time—dealing with peacekeeping authorization at the national level. The activities of the International Peace Academy (IPA), founded in 1971, have shown signs of more staying power. Following his retirement from the United Nations, General Rikhye served as the IPA catalyst for transnational projects seeking to bridge the gap between peace theory and peace practice. Taking advantage of the new impetus of United Nations forces in the Middle East, IPA scheduled in the summer of 1974 a workshop conference specifically designed to improve peacekeeping practices by bringing together military officers, civilian officials, and scholars with peacekeeping experiences or interests.

Despite the meagerness of continuing organizational research on peacekeeping forces, there is a substantial body of literature on a variety of peacekeeping issues.[4] The bulk of this literature is written by scholars interested in international relations, peace theory, and conflict resolution. The basic substance of these writings deals with the authorization, legal status, financing, and political backdrop of peacekeeping forces.[5] Overlapping with this literature are studies advocating greater reliance on international authority which sketch new forms of peacekeeping endeavors ranging from slight modifications of the existing capabilities of the United Nations to a supreme "one-world" policing army.[6] More concrete, though largely based on secondary analyses of documentary materials, are the detailed case studies of particular peacekeeping forces.[7] Another body of peacekeeping literature is that written by military officers with direct involvement or interest in peacekeeping forces.[8] Although such writings are not usually concerned with analytical issues, they do offer themselves as data sources.

The most sparse literature is that which deals directly with systematic analysis of peacekeeping forces. Issues in this literature include the exigencies bearing on military personnel which affect the development of minimal force precepts, political impartiality, and international identification.[9] Yet even this literature is mostly deduced from general principles or comparative analogy with standard national armies rather than derived from factual examination of actual peacekeeping forces. The number of empirical studies of UN peacekeeping soldiers—typically limited to post-peacekeeping interviews of soldiers from one nation—can be counted on one hand. Indeed, prior to the research employed for this monograph there has never been a full-fledged field study of a United Nations peacekeeping force.

Although the peacekeeping literature is voluminous and internally disparate and therefore not amenable to easy synthesis, our particular concerns are much more manageable. An interpretive reading of the literature does encounter certain recurring generalizations on the core issue of the military's adaptation to the peacekeeping role. These generalizations—or perhaps hypotheses —on the way in which the profession of arms relates to the peacekeeping endeavor can be summarized in the following inventory.

1. *Soldiers from neutral middle powers are more likely to subscribe to the constabulary ethic than soldiers from major powers.* This proposition is independent of and goes beyond the generally accepted principle that major powers are inappropriate participants in peacekeeping forces because of the considerations of international politics. The assumption here is that the military

personnel, themselves of neutral middle countries—those without traditions of aggressive warfare or embroilments on the international scene—will be most likely to display restraint and impartiality when charged with peacekeeping assignments. Conversely, the military establishments of major powers—with their historical and contemporary reliance on instruments of violence—will be least adaptable to the impartial and restricted use of force inherent in the peacekeeping mission. Put in another way, the political-military milieu of the contributing nation has a strong bearing on the propensity to use force on the part of the nation's soldiers.

2. *Soldiers from neutral middle powers are more likely to subscribe to international authority than soldiers from major powers.* With only some overstatement, the premise is that the citizens of neutral middle countries are less nationalistic than those from major powers. Because neutral middle countries possess a domestic political culture receptive to involvement in international bodies, such a political culture ought to have a positive effect on the propensity for international identification on the part of military personnel. Conversely, major powers, accustomed to playing a more independent international role, will be less likely to give up sovereignty to international bodies; military personnel from the major powers, coming out of this more parochial political culture, will be more reluctant to give higher allegiance to a United Nations body.

Here, as in the preceding proposition, a virtue appears to be made of a necessity—namely, the fortunate juxtaposition of availability *and* efficacy of forces from neutral middle powers for peacekeeping duties. That is, inasmuch as international constraints require that neutral middle powers serve as the primary reserve for peacekeeping forces, it may be too convenient that their military personnel are also those characterized as both least prone to use force and most likely to transcend national identities.

3. *Prior training of soldiers in peacekeeping skills will facilitate the development of the constabulary ethic among peacekeeping forces.* The thrust of this proposition proceeds from the not unwarranted assumption that traditional military training—whether in a major or minor power—seeks to socialize men into

the acceptance of violence, to develop skills in the use of lethal weaponry, and to promote the desirability of "victory" in the field. Contrarily, the skills of the peacekeeping soldier require such traits as the avoidance of violence, quiescent monitoring, negotiation, and compromise. It follows that substantial peacekeeping training and socialization in the anticipation of UN service is required to restructure the soldierly role away from reliance on coercive measures toward a model fostering the absolutely minimal use of force. Underlying this proposition is the belief that the ordinary soldier, conventionally trained, will encounter emotional as well as practical difficulties in adjusting to the peacekeeping role.

4. *Participation in a United Nations force will foster internationalist values on the part of peacekeeping soldiers.* Where the preceding propositions explained peacekeeping attributes on the basis of variables temporally antecedent to United Nations service (for example, values acquired by military personnel from neutral powers or prior peacekeeping training), the present proposition stresses causal processes on attitudinal change following and during assignment to a UN command. If the essential condition of conventional military socialization is loyalty to the nation-state, it follows that the peacekeeping soldier must be regeared toward a higher allegiance, at least while under the command of the United Nations. More directly, it is held that actual service as a UN peacekeeper will make one more of an internationalist. Something, that is, in the very performance of international missions linked with formal and informal socialization while under UN command will result in a reordering of national and international identities with the advantage to the latter. It should be recognized, however, that much of the writing on this point also entwines normative with descriptive assertions, such as the assertion that internationalist allegiances are of a higher order of legitimacy than national loyalties.

5. *The more internationalism exhibited by peacekeeping soldiers, the more the constabulary ethic will be displayed and vice versa.* Although the two variables of a constabulary ethic and internationalism have been purposely separated in the discussion here, they are almost always treated in tandem in the peace-

keeping literature. Indeed, a recurring theme of the writing on this topic is to posit a kind of peacekeeping "positive manifold" —the idea that internationalism and the constabulary ethic are similar components and go together. In fact, the lack of conceptual preciseness on this point is further evidence of confusion between descriptive and normative statements in much of peace theorizing. Inasmuch as both internationalism and avoidance of force are highly valued qualities among peace theorists, these values can too quickly translate into the theoretical premise that the two variables are twin facets of an overarching and indivisible peacekeeping factor. Thus a persistent lacuna in the extant peacekeeping literature is any acknowledgment of the empirical possibility that internationalism and the constabulary ethic are independently generated and have no necessary relationship to each other.

6. *Contemporary standards of military professionalism must undergo fundamental redefinition to meet the requirements of the peacekeeping role.* The premise here is that the disjunction between conventional armed forces establishments and peacekeeping requirements is so great as to necessitate a fundamental restructuring of the military profession if not its outright abandonment. Put briefly, the argument is that conventional military professionalism entails loyalty to the nation-state, expert command of lethal weaponry, and a willingness to employ that weaponry for chauvinistic purposes; peacekeeping professionalism requires internationalist identification, proficiency in noncoercive measures, and performance of mission in an impartial cause. Where military professionals are expert warriors serving national interest, peacekeeping professionals are an impartial and internationally legitimated constabulary. A corollary to this proposition is that peacekeeping missions will lead to a renaissance of the "professional pattern" within the military. It is perceived that the unity of the military organization with the nation-state so characteristic of modern history will begin to erode as peacekeeping demands increase.[10] The emergent organizational format of the armed forces will thus accommodate to military specialists with peacekeeping skills who can readily transfer their loyalties back and forth between national and international commands. Such a

development would be concurrent with and supported by the demise of the concept of the mass army in many postindustrial societies. It would encourage local disputants to submit to peacekeeping operations. Eventually it would create a new breed of international military peacekeeping professionals.

These six propositions capture the essentials of the literature dealing with the military aspect of peacekeeping forces. After we examine the formation, organization, and operation of the UN peacekeeping force in Cyprus, we will return to an explicit analysis of the specification and interrelationship of the factors affecting the peacekeeping role among military personnel. It can be noted even at this point, however, that, in the main, not one of these propositions concerning military peacekeepers is supported by the field research and inteview data to be presented.

This study, nevertheless, is not to be construed sheerly as an academic critique of the conventional wisdom concerning peacekeeping forces. Rather, the study suggests that peace theory unsupported by sociological data is liable to project certain idealizations on to what is an obdurate reality. More important, the present study is seen as part of the broader enterprise of encouraging the building of viable peacekeeping institutions. If the profession of arms is to become a major instrument of peacekeeping, its emergent qualities in this novel role must be approached through factually grounded analysis. Only in this manner can both theory and peace be served.

United Nations Military Forces: Background and Doctrine

2

A balanced and concise statement on the peacekeeping functions of the United Nations has been given by Inis Claude.[1] Peacekeeping is an interim measure, designed to forestall the globalization of a local conflict until a political solution can be devised and accepted. Peacekeeping represents an effort, not immediately to promote the settlement of disputes, but to prevent their degeneration into violent conflicts and thus to restore the possibility that practical settlements may be found. For the peacekeeping force, the positive objective of improving relations among parties already embroiled is subordinated to the negative purpose of preventing the entanglement of external powers. All United Nations peacekeeping forces have operated within the confines of a limited mandate. Or, to use a medical analogy, the military component of peacekeeping has been charged with a prophylactic role—the containment and retardation of conflict—rather than a therapeutic one—resolving the source of conflict. But rather than dwell on peacekeeping in the abstract, let us look briefly at the manner in which actual peacekeeping forces have been brought into being and have operated.[2]

The League of Nations

What appears to be the first concrete proposal to establish a peacekeeping force under the aegis and command of a genuinely international body (as opposed to a multinational allied force)

12

occurred in 1920. At that time there was a dispute between Poland and Lithuania over the status of Vilna in Poland. Although the city was Lithuania's historic capital, the majority of Vilna's inhabitants were Poles. With the concurrence of Poland and Lithuania, the League of Nations recommended a plebiscite in Vilna which was to be supervised by an international force. Ten nations (all European) agreed to contribute small contingents to what would be a 1,500-man League force. But by March 1921, owing to Lithuania's second thoughts, Soviet objections to an international force so close to its borders, and the reluctance of the contributing states to get involved in a foreign embroglio, the idea of the plebiscite was abandoned and with it the proposal of a League of Nations supervisory force. Nevertheless, the proposed Vilna force set a peacekeeping precedent by embodying the principle of a peacekeeping force instituted by a world organization.

The League's peacekeeping activities in the South American district of Leticia created a precedent of a different sort. In 1922, this virtually uninhabited 4,000 square mile area had been ceded to Colombia by Peru. A decade later, however, the dispute was reopened when Peruvian nationals from an adjacent region drove out the Colombian officials stationed in Leticia. The Peruvian government's opposition to Colombia's efforts to reoccupy the district led to minor skirmishes between the two nations. To prevent an outbreak of a full-scale war, the League of Nations proposed that Leticia be governed by a League commission while Peru and Colombia negotiated a settlement. The proposal was accepted by the concerned parties, and in June 1933 a League commission began its administration of Leticia. Upon the departure of the commission from Leticia in June 1934, the district was peacefully returned to Colombia. Significantly, from a peacekeeping standpoint, a seventy-five-man contingent of Colombian soldiers wearing the League armband was assigned to duty under the League commission. Thus, these seconded Colombian soldiers became, albeit in a marginal fashion, the first soldiers actually to be commanded by an international authority.

A much more significant example of the League of Nation's use of a peacekeeping force to settle a territorial dispute concerned the

Saar. In 1919, the former German area was placed under the administration of a League governing commission in which France initially had a dominant influence. The League's administration was to last fifteen years, at the end of which time the Saarlanders, almost all Germans, were to decide by plebiscite whether to rejoin Germany, pass to France, or remain under League control. Following the removal of the French garrison from the Saar in 1927, the international character of the governing commission became much more apparent. As the time for the plebiscite approached, the already highly charged local situation became aggravated by the belligerent German Nazi presence on the border. The governing commission requested an international force to maintain conditions of law and order before and during the voting. In December 1934, the first truly international peacekeeping force ever assembled arrived in the Saar. It consisted of thirty-three hundred officers and men: fifteen hundred from Great Britain, thirteen hundred from Italy, and two hundred fifty each from the Netherlands and Sweden. At the polls on January 13, 1935, over 90 percent of the Saarlanders voted for reunion with Germany. The international force, having successfully performed its mission, left shortly thereafter, and the Saar was reunited with Germany the following March.

The Saar international force was a remarkable accomplishment. Assembled only a month before the plebiscite and with no past experience to call upon, the force consistently operated in an efficient manner during its short tenure. Under the central command of a British major general, the force had a small British staff section complemented by English-speaking liaison officers in the Italian, Dutch, and Swedish contingents. Tactically, the force avoided deployment in small detachments and made its presence known to the population by frequent foot marches and vehicle patrols on major thoroughfares. Although troops were to come into action only at the request of the civil authorities of the governing commission, their use of weapons remained within the discretion of the military commanders. Official guidelines on the use of force were suitably pacific in tone but still sufficiently vague to allow latitude in interpretation, such as act with restraint, use only that force necessary to restore order.[3] Because of the general acceptance of the force on the part of the Saarlanders and the certainty of the plebiscite's outcome, however, there was never any instance in which the force had to resort to a show of arms. Nevertheless, what is important to note is that the League's international force in the Saar was employed in a military rather than police capacity.

Beside the proposals specifically involving peacekeeping forces mentioned here, the League of Nations, of course, took numerous other actions in situations that endangered the peace. Indeed, prior to 1930—before Japan, Italy, and Germany began their aggressive actions—the League's efforts to maintain peace were measurably successful. These generally took the form of fact-finding missions or "commissions of inquiry," which allowed the good offices of the League to serve as an instrument of conciliation between contending parties. But only in three instances—the proposed Vilna force, the pseudo-international Leticia force, and the Saar international force—did the League of Nations actually seek to establish a peacekeeping force that used military personnel.

The United Nations

With the founding of the United Nations in 1945, the prospects for international enforcement of peace seemed to revive. Unlike the defunct League, the new world organization was to have a credible military power under the provisions of chapter 7, articles 39–47, of the United Nations Charter. As originally envisioned in article 43, the member states of the UN were to make available to the Security Council the armed forces "necessary for the purpose of maintaining international peace and security." In practical terms, article 43 implied a permanent force (either in being or standby) which would fall under the command of the Security Council, in which each of the major powers had veto rights.

Furthermore, as authorized in article 47, a military staff committee, consisting of a representative from each of the Security Council's five permanent members, was to be responsible "for the strategic direction of the armed forces" and to assist the

Council on all questions pertaining to "military requirements for
the maintenance of international peace and security [and] the
employment and command of forces placed at its disposal." The
intent of article 47, then, was clearly to use "collective enforcement," as sanctioned by the major powers to deal with threats to
world peace. It was assumed that the major powers themselves
would provide most of the armed forces for the United Nations. It
is important to note that the collective enforcement provisions of
the original charter posited major-power coercion as distinct from
the twinned "peacekeeping" elements of noncoercion and
impartiality.

From the beginning, however, the military staff committee was
unable to operate in the intended manner. The growing cold war
between the United States and the Soviet Union dashed all hopes
that the two superpowers would continue their World War II
alliance into the postwar era. It soon became apparent that no UN
force could be directed by a committee, each of whose members
had a veto. Thus three decades after the framers of the Charter
sought to establish a permanent UN force, chapter 7 has never
been invoked for any purpose, and the military staff committee
has never played a role in any UN operation (although it still goes
through the motions of periodically meeting and adjourning).

When the Korean War broke out in June 1950, the United
States was successful in getting the Security Council—owing to a
temporary Russian boycott of the Council—to recommend that
member states come to the aid of South Korea and to invite the
United States, which had already deployed troops on the Korean
peninsula, to head a United Nations command. Nevertheless, the
United Nations presence in Korea can hardly be construed as an
example of an internationally sanctioned peacekeeping operation.
The misnamed "UN Command" in Korea never operated under
the direction of any United Nations body, nor was it financed in
any way from United Nations funds. In effect the Security Council
resolution served to legitimate the reality of the American
intervention on the side of South Korea in what became one of
the bloodier wars of this century.

In anticipation that the Soviet Union would not absent itself
again from Security Council deliberations, the United States in

1950 successfully sponsored the so-called "Uniting for Peace" resolution in the General Assembly. Passed over the objections of the Soviet-bloc minority, this resolution was an effort to give the veto-free Assembly a determining role in the authorization of United Nations military operations. In this way the United States, which at that time could command automatic majorities in the Assembly, sought to incorporate the UN in its anticommunist strategies. In subsequent maneuvers in the early 1960s, the United States also sought to enforce penalties on UN members who did not contribute to extraordinary peacekeeping expenses. This "Article 19 controversy" invoked the opposition of the strict constructionists—prominently the Soviet Union and France—who held that financial as well as other apsects of peacekeeping should be kept under the exclusive authority of the Security Council. By 1965, however, the United States had come to acquiesce in the view that no state could be compelled to support financially any peacekeeping operation of which it disapproved. In fact, as the Assembly membership became less and less malleable to American interests, the United States itself quietly abandoned the principles endorsed in the Uniting for Peace resolution. Thus, though coming at it from a different direction, the United States eventually found itself in agreement with the Soviet Union that prime determination for UN peacekeeping operations resided in the Security Council.

Another effort to overcome the failure of the military staff committee (under Security Council control) to authorize an internationalized UN military force was the 1948 proposal of Trygve Lie, the first secretary-general, to set up a permanent United Nations force recruited by the Secretariat. Lie's "UN Guard" initially envisioned a standing force of eight hundred international volunteers which would expand to as many as five thousand soldiers. The UN Guard would be used for guard duty with United Nations missions, the administration of truce terms, the supervision of plebiscites, and as a police auxiliary for cities like Jerusalem and Trieste when under international authority. Lie's proposal, however, encountered not only the expected opposition of the Soviet-bloc nations but also the lukewarm support, at best, of the United States and other Western countries. The final outcome, organizationally, was the establishment of a UN field service of unarmed international civil servants which provides administrative, clerical, and maintenance support for field missions. Nevertheless, the debate on Lie's proposal did indicate the beginnings of a United Nations consensus that peacekeeping ought to be removed from big-power participation and that the Secretariat should exercise greater initiative in the establishment and operation of peacekeeping forces.

Dag Hammarskjöld, who replaced Lie as secretary-general in 1953, sought to develop a peacekeeping machinery which could skirt the impasse over collective security procedures invested in the major powers of the Security Council. Under the guidance of Hammarskjöld, United Nations peacekeeping was to become a proper function of middle-sized powers with a commitment to political impartiality. These developments reflected both Hammarskjöld's broad definition of the Secretariat's peacekeeping responsibilities and the rapidly expanding and more heterogeneous membership of the United Nations. Moreover, even before Hammarskjöld, the United Nations had begun to acquire a peacekeeping record by monitoring cease-fires and performing related services on a variety of fronts.[4] These peacekeeping missions, though largely staffed with military personnel seconded to the United Nations from member states, were not properly a peacekeeping *force* inasmuch as they did not operate as a military organization or under military command. Typically, such peacekeeping observers were unarmed. Also, as "peacekeeping" was not a term in general use until the middle 1950s, these missions were at first simply labeled agents of "peaceful settlement," a designation which served to identify them with diplomatic rather than military activity.[5]

UNEF-1. The first employment of an international military force for UN peacekeeping occurred in the wake of the October 1956 attacks launched against Egypt by Israel, France, and Great Britain. Security Council actions to secure removal of the attacking forces were blocked by French and British vetoes. Consequently, with U.S. and Soviet concurrence, the provisions of the Uniting for Peace resolution were invoked, and the issue was transferred to the General Assembly. During the first week of November, the Assembly adopted a cease-fire resolution and authorized Secretary-General Hammarskjöld to recruit a United Nations military force composed of contingents volunteered by member nations. With the acquiescence of the disputants, a cease-fire went into effect and the Assembly created the United Nations Emergency Force (UNEF).

UNEF operated first as an interpositional force covering the withdrawal of the invasion troops. Subsequently, it served as a neutralizing presence by having nonfighting units patrol within Egypt along the Israeli borders in the Gaza Strip and the Sinai desert. At maximum strength in early 1957, UNEF consisted of six thousand officers and men drawn from ten countries: Brazil, Canada, Colombia, Denmark, Finland, India, Indonesia, Norway, Sweden, and Yugoslavia. Ten years later, UNEF consisted of thirty-five hundred soldiers from seven countries. For close to a decade UNEF served the purpose for which it was intended. But in May 1967, following Egypt's request for its termination, UNEF hastily withdrew at the secretary-general's order. This was to become one of the precipitating factors in the outbreak of the 1967 war in the Middle East. But, as Secretary-General U Thant and his principal peacekeeping adviser, Ralph Bunche, explained time and again, there was no legal way in which a UN force could remain in a territory against the will of a sovereign state. Nevertheless, the abrupt withdrawal of UNEF could not have failed to impair the credibility of United Nations peacekeeping arrangements.

ONUC. The largest and most controversial UN peacekeeping force was a product of the chaos that followed the attainment of independence by the Belgian Congo (now Zaire) in July 1960. Within two weeks of independence, the Congo suffered internal anarchy, the insurrections of its army, Belgian intervention, and the secession of its richest province, Katanga. The Congo central government requested help from the United Nations, and Secretary-General Hammarskjöld requested the Security Council to act urgently. The Council responded, with the United States and Soviet Union voting affirmatively, by authorizing the *Operation* *des Nations Unies au Congo* (ONUC) or the United Nations Congo Operation. The guidelines originally set forth by Hammarskjöld stipulated that ONUC could use force only in self-defense and forbade the UN troops to become a party to any internal dispute, that is, prohibited the use of armed force to end the Katanga secession.

The first UN troops arrived in the Congo on July 15, 1960; they were the precursors of a force which would eventually have over twenty thousand soldiers. Thirty-five countries contributed military personnel to ONUC, but the bulk of the soldiers came from ten African nations: Ethiopia, Ghana, Guinea, Liberia, Mali, Morocco, Nigeria, Sudan, Tunisia, and the United Arab Republic. Non-African states that also contributed sizable contingents were Canada, India, Indonesia, Ireland, and Sweden. A key airlift role in the early stages of ONUC was played by the United States. ONUC was always plagued by poor coordination of forces, conflicting goals between various national units, and a confusing dual civilian-military command system in which sometimes the secretary-general's special representative (a civilian official) and sometimes the supreme commander of the force (a senior general) each gave orders directly to the troops.[6]

Originally Hammarskjöld seemed to have in mind the termination of ONUC military activities as soon as the Belgian troops were removed and the Congolese army reestablished. After the murder of the Congolese prime minister, Patrice Lumumba, however, the Security Council, in February 1961, passed a new resolution which urged the United Nations to take "appropriate measures to prevent the occurrence of a civil war in the Congo, including ... prevention of clashes, and the use of force, if necessary, in the last resort."[7] On the initiative of the Special Representative, Conor Cruise O'Brien, the UN launched a full-fledged military operation against the Katanga secessionists in September 1961. However, Katanganese forces, allied with white mercenaries, inflicted a demoralizing defeat on ONUC, and the United Nations was forced to negotiate terms at a disadvantage. Dag Hammarskjöld himself was killed in an airplane crash while on these negotiations. The new secretary-general, U Thant, secured O'Brien's resignation, and the operations begun earlier in the month came to an end by September 20.

After September 1961, the UN gradually built up a stronger position in Katanga. In December of that year, reinforced UN troops coupled with air support occupied the major cities of Katanga. The UN offensive had broken the back of the Katanganese secessionist movement, and soon indigenous developments would lead to a modus vivendi among the Congo's political leaders. In appraising the UN's role in the Congo, it is obvious that what started out as a peacekeeping venture turned into a minor war. The canon of impartiality was clearly breached when ONUC employed armed force in support of the central government. Moreover, the United Nations had to bear tremendous financial burdens, suffered battle casualties, and even had some of its troops accused of committing atrocities. Nevertheless, by the time the last UN soldiers left the Congo in June 1964, ONUC had achieved definite results; it had preserved the territorial integrity of the Congo and had removed the country from the arena of cold-war confrontation.

UNFICYP. The third United Nations peacekeeping force arose out of a March 4, 1964, Security Council resolution unanimously recommending an international force to keep the peace in Cyprus. Internecine hostility between the preponderant Greeks and the minority Turks in the eastern Mediterranean island-republic erupted into violent fighting during Christmas week of 1963. Even more serious, a war between Greece and Turkey in support of their Cypriot compatriots was threatened. The immediate task of maintaining peace fell to the British, whose troops were already in Cyprus by treaty right and who maintained a large complex of bases on the southern part of the island. After attempts to reach agreement on a NATO peacekeeping force failed during the early months of 1964, the United Nations acted in March. The mission of the United Nations force defined by the 1964 Security Council resolution was "to use its best efforts to prevent a recurrence of fighting and, as necessary, to contribute to the maintenance and restoration of law and order and a return to normal conditions."[8] The first units of the United Nations Force in Cyprus (UNFICYP) arrived on the island in late March 1964. Subsequent renewals of the Security Council have kept the United Nations peacekeeping force in being through 1975.

At its peak strength in 1964, UNFICYP consisted of approximately sixty-five hundred soldiers, a force gradually reduced to twenty-three hundred men by 1974. Contributing nations of UNFICYP's military force have been: Austria, Denmark, Canada, Finland, Great Britain, Ireland, and Sweden. In accordance with arrangements worked out between the Secretariat and the Cyprus disputants, UNFICYP was instructed to interpose itself between the Greek and Turkish sides only when such interposition would be acceptable to the disputants; to negotiate in virtually all circumstances with the belligerents; and to restore freedom of movement throughout the island only when the right to do so had been secured by local agreements with Greek or Turkish Cypriots. Adopting in essence the mandate based on the UNEF precedent, UNFICYP was to use force only in self-defense and was thereby precluded from intervening militarily in the Cyprus dispute. Thus in several instances of fighting between Greek and Turkish Cypriots, UNFICYP either ineffectively stood by or, on at least one occasion, even abandoned its positions. Even though the potentiality for renewed conflict has remained a constant in volatile Cyprus, the island on the whole, due in some significant part to the United Nations presence, was characterized by relative calm for the ten years following UNFICYP's initial deployment. Thus, although the basic dispute between Greeks and Turks on Cyprus has remained unresolved, UNFICYP must be credited with some progress in its primary tasks of pacifying the Cypriot intercommunal war and reducing the likelihood of a major war between Greece and Turkey.

UNEF-2 and UNDOF. The fourth and fifth United Nations peacekeeping forces came about as a result of the biggest Arab-Israeli war in a generation. On October 6, 1973, Egyptian forces crossed the Suez Canal and Syrian forces attacked on the Golan Heights. After suffering initial losses, the Israelis mounted a counterattack and regained the initiative; following bitter conflict, a tenuous cessation of hostilities was reached by the month's end. After intensive diplomatic maneuvering between the United States, the Soviet Union, and the combatants, the Security Council passed an American-Soviet resolution on October 22 calling for a cease-fire in place. When the initial cease-fire in the Sinai failed to hold, Egypt proposed on October 24 that a joint U.S.-USSR force be sent to the Middle East to supervise the cease-fire. The U.S. rejected the proposal while the Soviets avoided a commitment one way or the other. On October 25, the world community was startled when America suddenly placed its military forces on a worldwide alert. For a moment the danger of a superpower confrontation was posed. The crisis abated as suddenly as it arose, when later that same day the U.S. and the USSR joined in passing a Security Council resolution establishing a new United Nations Emergency Force (UNEF) which excluded superpower participation.

By October 26, 1973, Secretary-General Waldheim had already formed the nucleus of the new UNEF, with advance elements coming from United Nations contingents in Cyprus. The total strength of UNEF was initially projected at seven thousand men. A UN troop strength of forty-five hundred men was realized over the next several weeks with contingents coming from twelve nations: Austria, Canada, Finland, Ghana, Indonesia, Ireland, Nepal, Panama, Peru, Poland, Senegal, and Sweden (domestic needs at home, however, caused the Irish contingent to be withdrawn in May 1974). Finnish Major General Ensio Siiasuvuo was appointed interim force commander. Pursuant to its mandate, UNEF has gone through three phases: first as an interposing force and observation element between the Egyptian and Israeli forces, later in controlling the separation and disengagement process, and eventually in manning the zone of disengagement (from base camps located on the Egyptian side).

While the October 1973 diplomatic efforts had been at least temporarily successful in separating Egyptian and Israeli forces, the situation on the Israel-Syria front was one of continued war. Aided by a virtuoso performance of U.S. secretary of state Henry Kissinger, an accord was finally reached in May 1974 which worked out a four-stage disengagement in the Golan Heights sector and the thinning of Israeli and Syrian military forces in that border region. To implement this arrangement, the Security Council on May 31, 1974, authorized the United Nations Disengagement Observer Force (UNDOF) and requested the secretary-general to take the necessary steps. Waldheim proceeded to organize a twelve hundred-man force, drawing from contingents already assigned to the recently formed UNEF. Peruvian Brigadier General Gonzalo Briceno Zevallos was appointed interim force commander, and by June 3, 1974, UNDOF was operational. Consisting of military units from Austria, Canada, Peru, and Poland, UNDOF was eventually to occupy a three-mile buffer zone in territory nominally under Syrian civil control.

While generally following the format of previous United Nations peackeeping forces, the authorizaiton of UNEF-2 and UNDOF broke new ground as well. The control of these peace-keeping forces was much more directly under the authority of the Security Council. Each step taken by the secretary-general to carry out the Security Council's mandate was to be submitted to the Council itself, including the appointment of force commanders and the national composition of the forces. Very important, the new UN peacekeeping forces in the Middle East would remain deployed as long as called for by their mandates—six months, initially, and subject to renewal thereafter. In effect, this meant that the withdrawal of the new peacekeeping forces could not be on the Secretariat's initiative but must remain the decision of the Security Council (although it was hard to conceive what could be done, practically speaking, if a contributing nation unilaterally withdrew from the peacekeeping force prior to the expiration of the mandate). Also, for the first time in peacekeeping history, a member of the Warsaw Pact, Poland, was included among the nations whose troops would take part in a United Nations operation.[9] Finally, in addition to their armed military components, both UNEF and UNDOF incorporated the services of unarmed military observers transferred from the United Nations Truce Supervision Organization (UNTSO) headquartered in Jerusalem. UNTSO, the longest-lived of any UN observation mission (in being since 1948), had since 1967 been monitoring the Suez Canal and Golan Heights with unarmed observers. It was anticipated that such unarmed military observers would be used extensively under UNDOF in the Golan Heights, especially in situations where there would be need for contacts with civilian populations.

Peacekeeping Doctrine

The formation of all five of the United Nations peacekeeping forces has occurred in the face of the inoperativeness of chapter 7 of the UN Charter, with its provisions for collective security enforced by the major powers. But this has led to the emergence of an alternate peacekeeping doctrine. The administrations of each of the secretary-generals have reflected varying political circumstances and personal styles and, consequently, varying modes of adaptation to the peacekeeping enterprise. During the secretaryship of Trygve Lie (1945–53), it early became apparent that U.S.-Soviet antagonisms would make inoperative the collective enforcement measures under Security Council control. Lie's subsequent proposal for a standing UN Guard was ill-conceived and drew support from no quarter. The situation of an anticommunist intervention in Korea under putative United Nations command, and the U.S. sponsorship of the Uniting for Peace resolution (giving peacekeeping authority to the General Assembly) could only exacerbate Soviet alarm—and that of other nations—over UN military forces. To further compound matters, the efficacy of the Secretariat was fundamentally impaired by Soviet perceptions of Lie's pro-Western stance.

With Dag Hammarskjöld at the helm (1953–61), the Secretariat interpreted its peacekeeping responsibilities most broadly and was the prime mover in the establishment of the first UNEF in the Middle East and the peacekeeping force in the Congo. In his well-known summary study of the the first UNEF experience, Secretary-General Hammarskjöld enunciated certain "basic principles" for peacekeeping forces: (1) the UN can station units in a territory only with the express consent of the government concerned; (2) the UN alone will decide the composition of its forces with due regard for the desiderata of the host country; (3) major powers should not provide contingents to the UN force; (4) the force must enjoy freedom of movement within the zone of operations; (5) UN personnel cannot be a party to any internal conflict and must maintain strict impartiality; (6) a UN force is an instrument for conciliation and cannot engage in combat activities, though it may respond with force to an armed attack in exercise of the right of self-defense.[10] These principles remain in the bedrock of UN peacekeeping doctrine.

Expanding upon the principles of the secretary-general's summary study, Lester Pearson, who as Canada's foreign minister won the Nobel Peace Prize as co-architect with Hammarskjöld of the first UNEF, set forth further elaborations for UN peacekeeping forces. According to Pearson, neutral middle powers ought to "earmark" military personnel or units in their national armies for possible UN duty, and such contingents should be prepared to perform "essentially noncombatant" tasks in their peacekeeping missions.[11] Since the formation of the first UNEF, about a dozen countries have actually earmarked forces for UN peacekeeping, although the level of preparedness of such forces varies considerably. But the peacekeeping role did make major headway in the national policies of several Western middle powers, most notably, Austria, Canada, Denmark, Finland, Ireland, Norway, and Sweden.

U Thant's secretary-generalship (1961–71) began inauspiciously with a constitutional crisis arising out of the financial burdens of the UN force in the Congo. A collision course between the U.S. and the Soviet Union—the "Article 19 controversy"—was avoided only when the principle was accepted that member states need not bear the obligations of peacekeeping operations to which they do not acquiesce. U Thant declined to imitate the pathbreaking ventures of his predecessor, and instead pursued a cautious course in exercising the Secretariat's peacekeeping responsibilities. Nevertheless, he was quite prepared to use energetically the Secretariat in the formation of UNFICYP. Moreover, notwithstanding the setback to the UN's peacekeeping credibility caused by his abrupt withdrawal of the first UNEF, U Thant fostered the practicality of United Nations peacekeeping by remaining on cooperative terms with all governments.

But it was also the case that, in the wake of the ONUC controversies, Thant was more careful than Hammarskjöld in seeing that the Secretariat's peacekeeping initiatives did not strain the political tolerances of the major powers. U Thant went on record as stating that he could foresee no possibility of establishing a permanent UN peacekeeping force in light of United Nations and international realities. He even stated that peacekeeping training for selected military personnel under UN auspices—a Hammarskjöld-Pearson proposal—was premature and impractical. Rather, Thant stressed reliance on a more modest program of improving procedures whereby member states would earmark elements of their armed forces for possible United Nations peacekeeping assignments.[12] It would be fair to state that where Dag Hammarskjöld was prone to take a peacekeeping initiative and then seek to build a consensus around it, U Thant was more likely to engineer a consensus before implementing peacekeeping actions.

The tenure of Secretary-General Kurt Waldheim (1972–) is yet too brief to warrant a definitive characterization. But it does seem likely that the strict constructionist interpretation of the peacekeeping prerogatives of the Secretariat followed by U Thant has been carried on by Waldheim.[13] Moreover, the Waldheim era will probably witness greater major-power involvement in the management of United Nations military forces through the mechanism of closer Security Council supervision. All this confirms a change in the peacekeeping role of the secretary-general. For those who saw in Hammarskjöld's initiatives the promise of an emerging international authority, it may seem like a step backward. But although Hammarskjöld's successors have seemingly been less versatile, they have nevertheless been more realistic in dealing with the prevailing power. Waldheim, furthermore, has revitalized the peacekeeping responsiveness of the Secretariat by appointing Brian Urquhart, who has succeeded Ralph Bunche as the world's champion of peacekeeping forces, as undersecretary-general. It also appears that the Secretariat's ability to conduct significant peacekeeping operations—the continuation of UNFICYP and the formation of UNDOF and the second UNEF—has been facilitated by the emerging U.S.-Soviet detente and the continued support of the middle powers.[14] As the United Nations approached its fourth decade, the conditions supportive of peacekeeping forces—if not of international peace—appeared to be gaining limited favor.

In sum, the institutional framework of peacekeeping forces is still in the process of definition. Peacekeeping soldiers have performed an arduous task and, with few exceptions, performed it well. The continued volatility of the areas to which they have been deployed, however, speaks too somberly of the limitations of United Nations forces. But the profession of arms in its latest incarnation, in the body of peacekeeping forces, may yet be destined to play a stabilizing role on the international scene.

UNFICYP: Formation and Mandate

3

Man has lived on Cyprus since before 5,000 B.C., and the island figures prominently in the antiquity of the eastern Mediterranean. The island (3,572 square miles) is 40 miles south of Turkey, 100 miles west of Lebanon, and 525 miles east of Athens. Sometime during the eleventh and tenth centuries before Christ, Cyprus became definitely Hellenic in ethnicity and culture. Despite repeated conquests and occupations by numerous foreign invaders, Cyprus still retains its essential Greek character and identity. However, one of the legacies of three centuries of Ottoman control (1571–1878) is a Turkish minority which today constitutes slightly under one-fifth of the island's 660,000 inhabitants. During the latter part of the Ottoman period, *enosis*, or union with the newly independent Greece, began to emerge as a rallying point for the majority Cypriot community.

It was not until after the British took over from the declining Ottoman Empire in 1878, however, that political demands for enosis became widespread. The period between the two world wars saw Cypriot Greeks, now articulating newly current ideas of self-determination, take political action, occasionally breaking out into violence, against British colonial rule. After a temporary abatement during World War II, agitation for enosis became even more virulent during the postwar period. In 1950 Archbishop Makarios III was elevated to the position of head of the Cypriot Orthodox church and ethnarch of the Greek community. Makarios was the latest in a long line of Cypriot archbishops who led the island's Greeks in both religious and political affairs. By the mid-1950s, the Greek government in Athens, under pressure from Makarios and its own domestic political situation, took a strong position in favor of the enosist demands of the Greek Cypriots. This in turn contributed to Turkey's adamant opposition to enosis and its projection as defender of Cypriot Turkish rights. Thus Great Britain's inflexibility in accommodating to Greek Cypriot demands was compounded by Greece and Turkey becoming locked into rigidly opposed positions on Cyprus.

In Cyprus itself, an underground organization, EOKA (an acronym from the Greek words for National Organization of Cypriot Fighters), under the leadership of the legendary Greek general George Grivas, opened a guerrilla offensive against the British. Although Makarios's control over the terrorist activities of EOKA is a matter of dispute, it is fair to say that the Archbishop dominated and directed the militant political campaign to oust the British.[1] While EOKA directed its terrorism against the British, enosis was also adamantly opposed by the island's Turks for whom it would mean becoming a tiny minority within Greece. Instead they proposed *taksim*, a kind of double enosis that would enable the Turkish sectors of the island to unite with Turkey and the Greek with Greece. They established a guerrilla unit of their own, TMT (Turkish Defense Organization). The worsening situation on Cyprus led to the British declaration of an emergency period (1955–59). All told, six hundred people died in the violence of those five years, and, as the emergency dragged on, the violence increasingly was between Greek and Turk as well as between Greek and Briton.

The bloody stalemate was finally broken by a series of diplomatic initiatives which led to conferences held in 1959 in Zurich and London. These Zurich-London Agreements, which underlay the establishment of an independent Republic of Cyprus, were signed by the prime ministers of Greece, Turkey, and Great Britain, by Dr. Fazil Kuchuk as the representative of the Turkish Cypriots, and by Archbishop Makarios, the most reluctant of the signers, representing the Greek Cypriots. The Zurich-London Agreements consisted of three treaties and the Cyprus Constitution. A "Treaty of Establishment" between Cyprus and Great Britain stipulated that the preexisting complex of British bases on the island would remain under British "sovereignty." A "Treaty of Guarantee" provided that Greece, Turkey, and Great Britain would guarantee the independence of Cyrrus with the proviso that enosis or partition would be forbidden. A "Treaty of Alliance" provided that Greece and Turkey, as guarantor powers, would station small troop-units on Cyprus.

The constitution authorized a republican form of government with a split executive: a Greek Cypriot president and a Turkish Cypriot vice-president, each of whom has veto rights. The constitution also detailed a form of proportional ethnic representation, favorable to the Turkish minority, for the legislature, the civil service, and the security forces. Large municipalities were to be governed under a form of communal autonomy. When Cyprus became independent on August 16, 1960, Makarios and Kuchuk became president and vice-president, respectively. The following month Cyprus was admitted to the United Nations as the ninety-ninth member of the world organization. In its subsequent UN voting record and other foreign policy actions, Cyprus has generally identified itself with a neutralist third-world viewpoint. In 1961 Cyprus applied and was accepted for membership in the British Commonwealth.

Greek Cypriot unhappiness with the Zurich-London Agreements was apparent even before independence. There was resentment of the limitations on Cyprus's freedom of action imposed by the various treaties and guarantee powers. More important, the constitutional system, with its extraordinary support of Turkish minority rights, generated apprehensions that the Greek majority would be unable to govern effectively. And in fact, implementation of key provisions in the constitution proved unworkable from the start. Agreements would not be made concerning the Turkish-weighted share of the civil service, the manner of integrating the two communities into the Cypriot army, and the establishment of communal councils in the large municipalities. Most serious, Turkish vetos prevented funds for the government from being collected or allotted. These deadlocks brought governmental machinery to a standstill, and communal violence flared again.

In November 1963 President Makarios proposed a list of

constitutional amendments to Vice-President Kuchuk and the guarantor powers. These were rejected by both the Turkish community in Cyprus and the Turkish government in Ankara. A few weeks later communal fighting developed into pitched battles between Greek and Turkish Cypriot irregulars. During Christmas week 1963 about one hundred persons were killed on each side. Turkish jets buzzed Nicosia on Christmas day. Peacekeeping machinery began to move, and, at the suggestion of the British government, Makarios agreed that a "tripartite" force of the three guarantor powers (Greece, Turkey, and Great Britain) would patrol Nicosia under British command. However, by the time this command was activated on December 27, the bulk of Greek and Turkish soldiers were already out of their camps manning strategic positions in support of the irregulars among their Cypriot co-ethnics. Thus the "triparite" peacekeeping force that began patrolling Nicosia was in effect a British operation that had been agreed to by the Makarios government. What had begun years earlier as an anti-British and anticolonial struggle, and had become an irreconcilable communal conflict between Cypriots, now threatened to lead to an intra-NATO war between Greece and Turkey.

During the last week of December 1963, British Commonwealth Secretary Duncan Sandys flew to Nicosia and after sessions with the disputants secured a number of important agreements. These included exchange of prisoners and hostages, and the creation of a British-patrolled "Green Line," or neutral cordon, to interpose British troops between the warring factions. The term "Green Line," which was to become a mainstay of Cypriot peacekeeping argot, originally derived from the color of the pencil used on British headquarters maps to demarcate the Turkish northern half of Nicosia from the Greek southern half of the capital city. The timely British intervention can be credited with forestalling full civil war between Greek and Turkish Cypriots. It is also generally acknowledged, however, that Great Britain's peacekeeping involvement in Cyprus was dictated by strategic concerns for her bases on the island.

By the end of 1963, the seven thousand British troops already stationed in the sovereign base areas were reinforced by another eleven hundred soldiers flown in from England and Libya, although only a fraction of this total complement was ever directly assigned peacekeeping tasks. By the spring of 1964, however, the British force had begun to lose the confidence of both Cypriot factions. The Turkish Cypriots complained that the British forces, by acting in a noncoercive manner, were ineffective in preventing the massacre of Turks by Greeks. The Greek Cypriots, for their part, were quick to recognize that the Green Line neutral zones throughout the island were partitioning the country, an occurrence which was anathema to the Makarios government in its efforts to impose a unitary state on the island.

Meanwhile, there was mounting alarm over a possible military intervention on the island by Turkey. The Cyprus representative to the United Nations called for a meeting of the Security Council, but no action was taken. In January 1964, Great Britain, Turkey, and Greece, with Makarios's approval, arranged for the secretary-general to assign a UN representative to Cyprus to observe the local situation and the peacekeeping efforts of the British troops. On January 16, U Thant appointed for this task Indian Lieutenant General Prim Singh Gyani, who had previously commanded both the UN emergency force in Suez and the UN observer group in Yemen. It was in this manner that the first United Nations presence appeared on the Cyprus scene.

The situation which General Gyani saw in Cyprus was one of rapid deterioration. During January and February of 1964, hostilities between Greek and Turkish Cypriots became more violent, with bombings, ambushes, and pitched battles being undertaken by each side. It was becoming apparent, moreover, that elements of the fighting forces were no longer under the effective control of their nominal communal leaders. Thousands of Turkish Cypriot families were leaving their home villages and moving to all-Turkish enclaves. The Cyprus government had come to mean the Greek Cypriot government when Vice-President Kuchuk and all the Turkish Cypriot ministers abandoned their offices. Pursuing a policy of unofficial partition, Turkish Cypriot leaders established their own de facto administration on the island and soon received the political and financial support of Ankara.

While the state of affairs in Cyprus approached anarchy and

predictions of a Greco-Turkish war were rampant, the British government proposed to Greece and Turkey, in late January 1964, that an international force made up of contingents from NATO countries replace the increasingly strained British force on Cyprus. Initially, the proposed force was to consist of ten thousand NATO troops (including American), to serve under British command. The concept of a NATO peacekeeping force revised to include non-NATO Commonwealth volunteers was acceptable to Greece and Turkey. But Makarios—fearful of a rerun of the major-power dictates of the Zurich-London Agreements—adamantly opposed such a force and held out instead for United Nations action. In the United Nations, presumably, the Makarios government would have had the more sympathetic support of the Asia-Africa bloc as well as of the socialist nations. Just exactly what Makarios wanted from the United Nations beyond the more sympathetic hearing for his position than he would receive in the councils of NATO is unclear. One writer has suggested that Makarios might have inadvertently engineered the UN peacekeeping force. That is, Makarios probably did not want a full-scale UN peacekeeping force in Cyprus but merely UN protection from Turkey so as to solve the island's communal problems by employing his own superior forces.[2] In any event, with the British determined to extricate themselves from an untenable position in Cyprus and with the Makarios government stymieing any NATO or Commonwealth approach, the time became opportune for a more direct United Nations role.

From mid-February through the first days of March 1964, the Security Council conducted extended debate on the Cyprus matter. Cyprus, Greece and Turkey, as nonmembers of the Security Council, and a spokesman for the Turkish Cypriot community were invited to participate in the Security Council debates. On March 4, 1964, the Security Council unanimously passed a resolution calling upon the secretary-general to establish a United Nations Peacekeeping Force in Cyprus—UNFICYP. However, in earlier voting, before the final adoption of the Security Council resolution, France, Czechoslovakia, and the Soviet Union announced certain reservations. All three nations went on record as objecting in principle to according the secretary-general so much of the Security Council's responsibility for a UN military force. Also, the two socialist members of the Security Council vigorously supported the initial position of the Cyprus government that the United Nations should, principally, protect Cyprus from outside intervention rather than authorize a domestic peacekeeping force. Nevertheless these objections had something of a pro forma nature, and the final resolution was accepted by all members of the Security Council.

The operative paragraphs of the Security Council resolution creating UNFICYP warrant citation in full:[3]

[The Security Council] *Recommends* the creation, with the consent of the Government of Cyprus, of a United Nations peacekeeping force in Cyprus. The composition and size of the force shall be established by the Secretary-General, in consultation with the Governments of Cyprus, Greece, Turkey and the United Kingdom. The commander of the force shall be appointed by the Secretary-General and report to him. The Secretary-General, who shall keep the Governments providing the force fully informed, shall report periodically to the Security Council on its operation.

[The Security Council] *Recommends* that the function of the force should be, in the interest of preserving international peace and security, to use its best efforts to prevent a recurrence of fighting and, as necessary, to contribute to the maintenance and restoration of law and order and a return to normal conditions.

[The Security Council] *Recommends* that the stationing of the force shall be for a period of three months, all costs pertaining to it being met, in a manner to be agreed upon by them, by the Governments providing the contingents and by the Government of Cyprus. The Secretary-General may also accept voluntary contributions for that purpose.

The March 4, 1964, Security Council resolution has been continually renewed over the subsequent decade and remains the basic mandate of UNFICYP. The original resolution also authorized the secretary-general to appoint a United Nations mediator to Cyprus who would use his good offices to work toward a peaceful settlement among the governments and communities involved. This position evolved into the secretary-general's special representative, a post held by a succession of distinguished international diplomats. Administratively speaking, the special representative was not part of the peacekeeping force, although in practice he worked closely with both civilian and military components of UNFICYP.

The Security Council resolution has several aspects worthy of comment. The mandate followed the pattern of those characterizing the first UNEF force and ONUC which gave the secretary-general wide latitude in mounting and running the peacekeeping operation. But it also specified that the force must be reauthorized by the Security Council in brief intervals—initially three months, later six months—thus keeping the secretary-general on somewhat of a short leash. Moreover, there was the requirement that the peacekeeping force not be a charge to the United Nations budget (though the costs of the special representative were chargeable to the UN budget). The financial needs of the force—(US) $165 million from 1964 to 1974—have been met by voluntary donations (close to 40 percent coming from the United States), with some costs being borne by nations contributing troop units to UNFICYP (principally the United Kingdom and Canada).[4]

Upon the passage of the Security Council resolution, Secretary-General U Thant took immediate steps to field a peacekeeping force in Cyprus. The provisional goal was a maximum force of seven thousand men, half of whom were already assured by a British commitment. Thus, even though a permanent member of the Security Council, Great Britain became a mainstay of the UNFICYP operation. Moreover, the British sovereign base areas—locally referred to as the "SBA's"—were to serve as a logistical backup for UNFICYP. In addition to the British, five other national contingents coming from Canada, Denmark, Finland, Ireland, and Sweden were placed under UNFICYP command. These non-British units arrived in Cyprus in mid-March, and UNFICYP was declared operational on March 27, 1964. Also, from the start of UNFICYP, Austria contributed a military hospital unit which could offer medical support for three thousand men (the British contingent relied on the medical facilities of their sovereign bases). In 1972, after making necessary changes in its constitution, Austria sent a regular military contingent to UNFICYP as well.

At its peak strength in 1964, UNFICYP consisted of slightly under sixty-five hundred soldiers. From 1965 to 1968, UNFICYP troop strength averaged around forty-five hundred, from 1969 to 1972 about thirty-five hundred, and in 1973 and 1974 about twenty-five hundred soldiers. Generally speaking, the reduction in UNFICYP troop strength over the years was proportionate to the initial numbers of the contributing nations, although in the spring of 1973 the Irish contingent was drastically cut back to company size. By late 1973, the Austrian military hospital was replaced by a smaller UNFICYP medical center with Austrian doctors in attendance. Also coming under the command of UNFICYP was a civilian police force—UNCIVPOL—which remained at a constant strength of about one hundred seventy-five men from 1964 to 1974. UNCIVPOL consisted of police volunteers from Australia, Austria, Denmark, and Sweden (additionally, New Zealand participated in UNCIVPOL from 1964 to 1967).[5]

Under the terms of its status-of-forces agreements, UNFICYP was authorized to deploy throughout Cyprus with putative freedom of movement. But the mandate of UNFICYP was vague enough to allow the disputants to read their own self-serving interpretations into it. For the mainland Turkish government and the Turkish Cypriot community, UNFICYP's tasks were to enforce the Cyprus Constitution that resulted from the Zurich-London Agreements, or at least to protect the Turkish enclaves on the island. For their part, Greek Cypriots saw the UNFICYP mandate as assisting the Cyprus government to put down a seditious Turkish community, or at least to enforce the central government's writ throughout the island. Though this ambiguity in UNFICYP's mandate could and did lead to problems in the field, it helped to make the UN force acceptable to the concerned parties. It is also important to note that, from the beginning, UNFICYP was outmanned and outgunned by other military forces on the island—Greeks, Turks, Greek Cypriots and Turkish Cypriots. Any one of these groups of well-led and well-trained armed men could present itself as a very real obstacle to the tactical operation of UNFICYP.

Thus UNFICYP has been circumspect in its utilization of force or even the threat of force and has instead relied—for practical reasons as well as from a principled reluctance to use coercion—on mediation, persuasion, and other peacekeeping skills. The successes and limits of the peacekeeping force in following its mandate can be summed up under headings from the Security Council's enabling resolution.

Prevent a recurrence of fighting. The first need was to stop the Greek and Turkish Cypriots from fighting and killing each other. In what U Thant called a "process of 'de-confrontation,' " UNFICYP elements were interposed between the opposing camps.[6] In urban areas this usually involved close patrolling of the Green Lines separating Greek from Turkish quarters. In the countryside, UN-manned outposts occupied visible positions on the periphery of Turkish Cypriot enclaves. Normally these UNFICYP units monitored the activities of the opposing armed elements with special attention on reporting improvements of fortifications and troop movements. In the event of such escalatory activities, the United Nations headquarters tried to persuade the offending party to return to the earlier status quo or tried, even, to increase the distance between armed Greek and Turkish Cypriot forces.

More serious were shooting incidents across the de facto borders dividing the two communities. Sometimes with malice aforethought, but more frequently as the result of perceived immediate provocation, such shooting often escalated into volleys back and forth with attendant casualties. Upon an outbreak of shooting, UNFICYP would first try to arrange a cease-fire and then conduct an investigation intended to lead to the identification—and, it was hoped, punishment by the communal leadership—of the initial violator. Over the past decade, though with generally decreasing frequency, there have been hundreds of shootings, nearly all of which resulted in UNFICYP investigations and reports.

Having graver potential than unpremeditated shootings were

incidents involving planned ambushes or confrontations between Greek and Turkish Cypriot armed elements. Three such occurrences reveal the varying levels of UNFICYP's peacekeeping potential and limitations. One incident developed out of the announcement in November 1965 by the Greek Cypriot government that it would build coastal defenses adjacent to the Turkish quarter of the port city of Famagusta. The fortifications, the government argued, were for defense against external invasion. The Turkish Cypriots, as expected, regarded the planned fortifications as a direct threat and hastily prepared new military positions of their own. An armed confrontation seemed imminent. After much negotiation UNFICYP got the Greek Cypriots to agree to abandon their plans for coastal defenses and convinced the Turkish Cypriots to remove themselves from their newly dug-in positions.

Another incident occurred in the village of Arsos when, in September 1966, a Turk cycling home was shot dead without apparent reason. Tension immediately rose, and a small UNFICYP detachment moved into the village. Two days later a Greek was killed in a retaliatory shooting. Shooting continued sporadically, endangering both the UNFICYP soldiers and the villagers. Finally, UNFICYP troops entered the houses from which the firing was originating and verbally ordered the snipers to lay down their arms. Fortunately they did so; had the snipers refused, the UN soldiers would have been unable to do much about it.

The most serious incident to confront UNFICYP occurred in November 1967, in Ayios Theodoros, where the situation was extremely tense owing to the Greek Cypriot government's attempt to expand its police patrols into the Turkish sector of that village. Evidence points to the Turkish Cypriots as having opened fire, and this became the signal for a preplanned, all-out assault on the Turkish quarter by a large Greek Cypriot force. In a sharp battle, about thirty Turkish Cypriots were killed as well as several Greek Cypriots. During the incident, UNFICYP positions were overrun by advancing Greek Cypriots, UNFICYP troops were manhandled and forcibly disarmed, and United Nations facilities were destroyed. In response to the Turkish Cypriot losses, Turkey began mobilizing its military machine, threatening invasion of either or both Cyprus and mainland Greece. Intense diplomatic efforts ensued, involving representatives of the United Nations, the United States, and NATO who shuttled back and forth between Nicosia, Athens, and Ankara. These diplomatic exchanges, coupled with a reasonably effective United Nations supervised cease-fire in the Ayios Theodoros area, succeeded in defusing the situation. But not before it again had been demonstrated how a local outbreak of violence on Cyprus could bring the eastern Mediterranean to the brink of war.

After Ayios Theodoros, when the Greek and Turkish Cypriots and their mainland patrons had looked into the abyss, premeditated armed clashes between the two sides virtually came to an end. The calmer atmosphere which prevailed between Greek and Turkish Cypriots after 1967, however, was also coterminous with outbreaks of political violence *within* the Greek Cypriot community. General Grivas, who had been recalled to Greece in 1967 only to return surreptitiously to Cyprus in 1971, was now accusing President Makarios of betraying the enosist cause. Indeed, whatever the degree of President Makarios's and the Cyprus government's continuing commitment to the ideal of enosis, there was a realistic recognition after the 1976 confrontation that any attempt to achieve union with Greece could well lead to war with Turkey. Moreover, Makarios's support from the locally powerful Greek Cypriot Communist party—always cool to enosis —only added to the frustration of the Greek hypernationalists on Cyprus. Grivas and his supporters formed a new underground organization—EOKA-B—which was dedicated to press the unionist cause relentlessly and to depose Makarios. Starting in the early 1970s, enosist diehards raided police stations, kidnapped and harassed Makarios supporters, and even attempted to assassinate Makarios himself.

President Makarios's position was further threatened by the fact that the officers of the Cypriot National Guard—the Greek Cypriot army—were mainland Greeks whose loyalty to the "Hellenic center" in Athens far outweighed any desire to preserve the independence of Cyprus. Increasingly worried about the reliability of the Cypriot National Guard, Makarios created a counterweight by organizing a personally loyal tactical police brigade. In January 1974, Grivas died (of natural causes).

Whether the demise of the old general would lead to a fragmentation of EOKA-B, or whether the enosist cause would find more effective leadership in younger firebrands, was hard to predict. Although internal Greek quarrels did not directly affect UNFICYP in either its field operations or mandate, United Nations officials were necessarily apprehensive that the internecine Greek conflict could upset the fragile peace between the Cypriot Greek and Turkish communities. At the least, the growing political instability on the Greek side of Cyprus could only complicate the peacekeeping mission.

Contribute to the maintenance and restoration of law and order and a return to normal conditions. Where the first category of UNFICYP activities were of a pacification nature, the second set of UNFICYP activities involved normalization measures, that is, amelioration of the political, administrative, and economic difficulties caused by the rupture between Greek and Turkish Cypriots. Following the outbreaks of violence in late 1963, there was to be a five-year period of virtually no contact between the two communities. During this period the only channel of communication took place through the mechanism of the UNFICYP Political Liaison Committee, which met separately in biweekly sessions with military officers representing the Cyprus government and the Turkish administration.

In June 1968, however, under the prodding of the secretary-general's special representative, direct negotiations between Greek and Turkish spokesmen began. These discussions were headed by two lifelong friends: Glefkos Clerides, president of the Cyprus house of representatives and nominal vice-president of the Greek Cypriot community; and Rauf Denktash, who had succeeded Kuchuk as leader of the Turkish Cypriot community and was to be elected constitutional vice-president of Cyprus in 1973. Nevertheless, the results of the off-and-on Clerides-Denktash negotiations were inconclusive as of 1974. The parties remained stymied on resolving Greek Cypriot demands for a unitary state and Turkish Cypriot insistence for federal autonomy. As a gesture, however, the Cyprus government did grant Turkish Cypriots limited access to civilian airport and seaport facilities, and allowed some Turkish Cypriots to seek employment in the Greek sector.

But the paramount social reality continually confronting UNFICYP was the division of the island into two de facto communal states. On the one side was the majority Greek sector, in charge of the central government and controlling about 90 percent of the island's territory. Since 1965 the Greek sector had experienced an economic boom, was administered by an efficient civil service, developed an impressive array of urban and rural services, and maintained parliamentary forms though increasingly torn by internal political disputes. Relations between the Greek Cypriot government and the mainland government in Athens fluctuated but with a definite trend toward increasing estrangement. On the other side were the refugee-swollen Turkish enclaves in the countryside and the Turkish quarters in municipalities and major villages. The largest of these enclaves consisted of most of the old city of Nicosia and a hinterland to the north from which the Turkish Cypriot administration retained a tenuous hold on isolated Turks in other areas. Since the division of the island, the Turkish sector had become economically stagnant; it suffered a deterioration in public services but nevertheless maintained a communal identity and a united front in its negotiations with the Cyprus government. The Turkish government in Ankara consistently followed a policy of close political and financial support of the Turkish Cypriot administration.

In this political environment, UNFICYP was the solitary link between the leaderships of the two communities from 1964 to 1968. Even since that time, UNFICYP has remained a prime communication channel for the normalization of Cypriot life. The tracing of missing persons and the securing of the release of hostages have been among the major accomplishments of the good offices of UNFICYP. Moreover, largely through the forum of indirect negotiation offered by UNFICYP, public services such as telephone, electricity, water, and the postal system returned to normal throughout most of the island. In its early years UNFICYP alleviated the plight of the Turkish Cypriot refugees by supervising the relief efforts of the International Red Cross and the Red Crescent Society of Turkey. UNFICYP personnel took direct part in the provision of relief supplies in the form of food and medical aid and in the building of schoolrooms for the refugee children. Also, UNFICYP has been successful in persuading the Cyprus government to expand its list of exceptions to the economic blockade of the Turkish enclaves.

Almost from its inception UNFICYP regarded the restoration of traffic patterns as a vital requisite of normalizing Cypriot daily life. Escort services were provided for persons—schoolchildren, maintenance workers, farmers—traveling in areas where they might be subject to attack or intimidation. It has been a standing UNFICYP policy to reduce these escort services as quickly as practicable and thus to establish a network of normalization precedents. The most routinized transportation service provided by UNFICYP has been its twice-daily escort of Greek Cypriot civilian vehicles through the major Turkish enclave between Nicosia and the northern seacoast town of Kyrenia. The "Kyrenia convoy" which started out with heavily armed UNFICYP vehicles interspersed throughout the convoy and UNFICYP guards along the roadway has since become reduced to a symbolic United Nations jeep leading the convoy.

The United Nations civilian policy force in Cyprus (UNCIVPOL) is a nonmilitary component of UNFICYP specifically detailed to normalization activities. Scattered in seven stations throughout the island, UNCIVPOL personnel are the constabulary peace-keepers par excellence. They have no direct powers of arrest, search, or interrogation. They can detain no one and cannot disperse unlawful crowds. They go about their duties unarmed, though for most of them it was normal practice to carry side arms in their home countries. What UNCIVPOL can do is to observe, investigate, and report on the suspicion of civil criminal acts. It can also, if requested by the Greek or Turkish Cypriot authorities, appear and testify in court. In actuality, UNCIVPOL duties are to serve as liaison between Greek and Turkish Cypriot civil policemen in cases involving nonpolitical crimes committed across communal boundaries. In the normal run of events, UNCIVPOL deals with such crimes as predial larceny, common thefts, broken contracts, and the like. (It must also be acknowledged that, in addition to its manifest police functions, UNCIVPOL acts as an unofficial intelligence arm of UNFICYP.) That, despite the division of the island, there has been little countenancing of cross-communal crimes by either Greek or Turkish Cypriots must in some measure be credited to the constabulary role played by the United Nations civilian policemen.

One of the most novel undertakings of UNFICYP was to promote a return to normal economic conditions. This goes much beyond its early tasks of assisting displaced persons or escorting endangered farmers to fields and markets. Shortly after its inception, UNFICYP established an economics section which has played a major role in the restoration and maintenance of the agricultural economy of Cyprus. By serving as a broker between farmers who abandoned their lands and the opposite communal group occupying those lands, UNFICYP has seen that rent payments are made to title-owners and that irrigation fees are settled with water authorities. In addition to its normalization of agricultural activities, UNFICYP has served as a go-between for Greek and Turkish Cypriot businessmen, conducted property-damage surveys, evaluated rebuilding programs, combatted forest fires, and arranged for reopening factories, kilns, and bakeries. A decade after it was first called to Cyprus, the United Nations force remained the only channel through which Greeks and Turks could negotiate over land and water rights, sale of crops, and numerous other commercial activities.

With regard to its dual goals of pacification and normalization, the record of the United Nations peacekeeping force in Cyprus is impressive. Except in a few isolated instances, the personnel of UNFICYP have consistently displayed impartiality in inter-communal embroilments and a noncoercive approach in the implementation of their mandate. The decline of violence on the island and the restoration of everyday life to something approaching normality must in some significant measure be credited to UNFICYP. These happy developments, however, must not obscure the fact that UNFICYP's effectiveness is ultimately limited by the willingness of the Cypriot communities to accept and utilize the offices and legitimacy of the United Nations force. Moreover, when other than pacification and normalization issues are involved, the root decisions regarding war and peace rest with the principal parties: the Cyprus government, the Cypriot Turkish administration, and beyond to Greece and Turkey.

Even though the potential for renewed violence remains a constant, the central fact is that UNFICYP has calmed the Cypriot communal war and staved off a Greco-Turkish international war. It has been a positive example of what a peacekeeping force is supposed to be and of how it should operate. After a full decade, whatever happens, UNFICYP's credit in this regard is clear.

UNFICYP: Organization and Operation

4

The information for this study of United Nations military peace-keepers is based primarily on field research conducted in Cyprus over an eight-month period during 1969–70. And unless otherwise stated all documentary material and statistical data presented herein refer to UNFICYP conditions as they existed in early 1970. The period of the field research was a rather typical one for UNFICYP's organization and operation. The chain of command system and the zones of responsibility of the contingents had been more or less consistent since 1965. Moreover, since the Ayios Theodoros battle of 1967, UNFICYP's pacification and normalization missions had evolved into routinized standards of procedure. Thus, all in all, the time of the field research was fortuitous precisely because of the very ordinariness of the peace-keeping situation.

Formal Organization

UNFICYP in 1970 consisted of about 200 civilians and 3,500 military personnel. The civilian side included an official staff of about ten persons: political and legal advisers, an administrative section, a chief of general services, a procurements representative, and a public information officer. The ranking civilian official of UNFICYP was the senior political and legal adviser. Also playing an important role—though technically not an UNFICYP official and with an unclear protocol relationship to the senior political and legal adviser—was the secretary-general's special representative. All UN civilian officials were serving indeterminate tours in Cyprus. Another twenty or so civilians on routine UN field service assignments acted as secretaries, radio operators, or drivers for the UNFICYP staff. There were also the 175 civilian police officers—UNCIVPOL—who were directly under the UNFICYP military command structure. A complete account of the civilian component must also mention the three to four hundred local Cypriot employees chiefly engaged in maintenance and kitchen duties, who though not members of UNFICYP were nevertheless on the United Nations payroll.

It was the military side, however, which was by far the numerically dominant component of UNFICYP and which gave the United Nations presence in Cyprus its distinguishing quality. The head of the United Nations force in Cyprus was the force commander, a position which has existed in all UN peacekeeping forces, and was directly appointed by the secretary-general. Indian Lieutenant General Prim Singh Gayani was designated the first force commander of UNFICYP. General Gayani, who had been on the island since January 1964 as the secretary-general's observer, accepted U Thant's appointment on the condition of serving only three months. On July 8, 1964, another Indian general, Kadendera Sabbayya Thimaya, assumed the position of force commander. General Thimaya died suddenly on December 18, 1964, and UNFICYP's chief of staff, British Brigadier A. James Wilson, was named acting commander. On May 17, 1966, Wilson reverted to chief of staff, when Finnish Major General Ilmari Armas Martola was named to command the United Nations force. Upon General Martola's retirement on December 20, 1969, the secretary-general appointed Major General D. Prem Chand as force commander, the third Indian general to head UNFICYP.

The force commander's role was spelled out only weeks after UNFICYP became operational. In an April 11, 1964, aide mémoire, Secretary-General U Thant stipulated that the force commander was not to act as a broker seeking to coordinate independent contingent commanders in some kind of joint operation.[1] Rather, the force commander was to be directly in command of all units, including UNCIVPOL; the contingent commanders were subordinate to UNFICYP command and were not to receive instructions from their home countries. And in fact there seems to have been relatively little friction between the secretary-general and his force commander, or between the force commander and the contingent commanders. By and large, the peacekeeping force in Cyprus has been characterized by successful control/command arrangements: an essentially nondirective Security Council, the delegation of substantial authority to the secretary-general for the definition and direction of the peacekeeping force, and a force commander heading a unified command solely responsible to the secretary-general.[2]

The force commander, while not directly in charge of the civilian staff, occupied a kind of first-among-equals position with regard to the senior political and legal adviser. The force commander's protocol relationship with the special representative was even more ambiguous inasmuch as both men reported directly to the secretary-general. The inherent likelihood for conflict in undefined relationships such as these between the force commander and high UN officials—in and out of Cyprus—can be mitigated to the degree that there are informal understandings and mutually tacit recognitions of respective prerogatives. Although UNFICYP appears to have had generally smooth relationships between the force commander and civilian officials in the UN hierarchy, such has not always been the case in other peacekeeping forces.[3]

The formal structure of UNFICYP is illustrated in figure 1 and the troop strengths of its various components are listed in table 1. The table of organization presented here is an outcome of my own research on UNFICYP's formal structure and differs in minor detail from that officially in use at the time of the field research. It has been related to me on good authority, however, that subsequently a new table of organization was drafted which relied in part on my emendations. In any event, it is the force commander who directly commands the civilian police force of UNCIVPOL and the national contingents from Great Britain, Canada, Denmark, Finland, Ireland, and Sweden; in UNFICYP nomenclature these were termed, respectively, Britcon, Cancon, Dancon, Fincon, Ircon, and Swedcon. The six national contingents, organized

Fig. 1. Organization Chart of UNFICYP, 1970

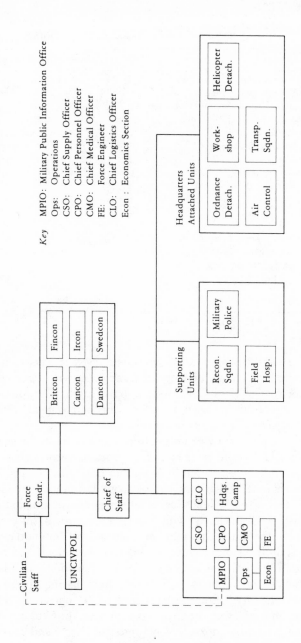

Key MPIO: Military Public Information Office
     Ops: Operations
     CSO: Chief Supply Officer
     CPO: Chief Personnel Officer
     CMO: Chief Medical Officer
     FE: Force Engineer
     CLO: Chief Logistics Officer
     Econ : Economics Section

Table 1. UNFICYP Troop Strength by Component, January 1970

Component	Officers	Other Ranks	Total
Headquarters Staff (multinational)	38	145	183
Headquarters attached units: ordnance, air control, workshop, transportation, helicopter detachment (Great Britain)	15	192	207
Britcon (Great Britain)	32	577	609
Cancon (Canada)	38	498	536
Dancon (Denmark)	60	415	475
Fincon (Finland)	46	419	465
Ircon (Ireland)	39	370	409
Swedcon (Sweden)	43	354	397
Supporting units military police (multinational)	5	60	65
field hospital (Austria)	12	40	52
reconnaisance squadron (Great Britain)	6	120	126
Total	334	3,190	3,524

SOURCE: UNFICYP personnel roster.

along the lines of infantry battalions, averaged between four hundred and six hundred men each and collectively made up over 80 percent of UNFICYP's total troop strength. The force commander has always been a two- or three-star general, with the contingent commanders being colonels.

Operating directly below the force commander in the chain of command was the chief of staff, a brigadier general, who was responsible for the various staff sections of UNFICYP. The headquarters staff, which consisted of about 180 military personnel, was made up of the following: a military public information office (which worked closely with UNFICYP's civilian information office), the camp headquarters, signals or communications, medical officer, force engineer, logistics, personnel, and operations. The operations section was the most important and largest section of the military staff. Apart from having the task of preventing new outbreaks of fighting, the operations section served in liaison with the Cyprus government, the Cypriot Turkish administration, and the national forces of Greece and Turkey.[4]

As reported in table 2, the officer component of the head-quarters staff was a genuinely international body, drawing its membership from the national contributors to the UNFICYP force. The proportion between officer groups from the different countries was approximately the same as that between the national contingents. From each country there was at least one staff officer of the rank of lieutenant colonel. Among other ranks,* however, the UNFICYP staff reflected a large predominance of British military clerks.

The staff organization of UNFICYP resembled in basic respects that of any operational military force, with two major exceptions. One was the absence of a formal intelligence section (primitive intelligence of a sort was conducted through a subsection of the operations office). This organizational feature was the result of a standing United Nations policy that it is impolitic to have a formal intelligence arm in peacekeeping operations.[5] The second exception was the existence of an economics branch under operations. As discussed earlier, the economic activities of UNFICYP were novel tasks for military personnel but, neverthe-

Table 2. UNFICYP Headquarters Staff by Nationality and Rank, January 1970

Nationality	Officers	Other Ranks	Total
Austria	1	0	1
Canada	5	24	29
Denmark	5	3	8
Finland	4	1	5
Great Britain	14	114	128
Ireland	4	2	6
Sweden	5	1	6
Total	38	135	183

SOURCE: UNFICYP staff list.

*The term "other ranks" is used in this study to refer to all soldiers other than commissioned officers. In American usage this corresponds to the term "enlisted men," including sergeants. "Other ranks" is preferred here because it is the terminology adopted in United Nations peacekeeping forces as well as standard English usage outside of the United States.

less, had come to play a continuing and effective role in the normalization of Cypriot everyday life.

Also located at the headquarters base and operating directly under the control of the chief of staff were small operational and maintenance units seconded to UNFICYP from Great Britain. These attached units, about two hundred soldiers in all, were used in an ordnance detachment, a workshop, a transportation squadron, an army air-control unit, and a helicopter detachment. Along with the British-manned components of the logistics section (movement control, and electrical and mechanical engineers), this gave a decidedly British cast to the everyday activities of the UNFICYP headquarters infrastructure.

In addition to the national contingents, the headquarters staff, and attached British elements, there were three other supporting units that completed the UNFICYP military table of organization. One was a 125-man British armored car reconnaissance squadron on alert to be moved anywhere on the island in time of crisis. Located in the Britcon zone, the reconnaissance squadron was the most "combat ready" of all of UNFICYP's forces and made routine morale-boosting visits to outlying United Nations positions. A second supporting unit was the Austrian field hospital; a 50-man military unit including nine erstwhile civilian doctors and dentists fulfilling their Austrian military obligations. The field hospital had the responsibility for treating UNFICYP soldiers—except those in Britcon, which relied on medical facilities in the British sovereign bases—whose ailments or wounds could not be handled by national contingent medical officers. The field hospital also offered free dental care, a service much used by UNFICYP personnel. The professional competence of the field hospital medical staff was highly regarded throughout UNFICYP.

The third supporting unit of UNFICYP, the military police company, requires special comment. "M.P. Coy" consisted of sixty soldiers drawn from each of the six national contingents and was the only international military unit in UNFICYP except for the headquarters staff.[6] Mixed national patrols of military policemen were very evident in the Nicosia area (though other zones were generally patrolled by M.P. Coy soldiers of the same nationality as the local contingent). The legal powers of the UNFICYP military police derived from a maze of documents: the Status-of-Forces agreement between the United Nations and the Cyprus government, which authorized the military police role; UNFICYP standing operating procedures, which stated general guidelines for the military police company; and the standing orders of the military police company, which spelled out in close detail the prerogatives of the UNFICYP military policeman. With regard to Cypriot civilians, UNFICYP military police had no authority to arrest, but they could search Cypriots entering and leaving UNFICYP facilities and could take into temporary custody any person causing a disturbance on United Nations premises.

The primary responsibilities of the United Nations military police, of course, were not with civilians but with UNFICYP soldiers. The military police company had jurisdiction over all United Nations soldiers outside the camps of their respective contingents. A special investigations section of M.P. Coy dealt with major incidents—unnatural death, sexual offenses, black market activities, serious theft, and so on. But the routine duties of the UNFICYP military policeman—as with his more conventional counterpart in national armies—concerned traffic violations, unauthorized absences, curfew violators, barroom squabbles, and venereal disease control. The military police company, while authorized to make arrests, had no powers of punishment; violators were handed over to their national contingents for disciplinary action.

A suspect returned to his national contingent was tried and punished in accordance with the military justice standards of his nationality. Minor infractions of soldiers from headquarters or from M.P. Coy itself were handled by the highest ranking officer from the unit of the offender's nationality; if the offenses were more serious, the offender was sent to the appropriate national contingent for punishment.[7] Thus, in no instance could a soldier be punished by a military officer of other than his own nationality. Generally speaking, routine violations met with either fines or restriction to quarters within the UNFICYP contingents. More serious discipline problems in Dancon, Fincon, and Swedcon were immediately sent home for disposition in civil courts; while Britcon, Cancon, and Ircon would punish the man in the unit in Cyprus, or in very severe cases return the man to a military prison in the home country.

Because every UNFICYP soldier was ultimately subject only to the laws of his own national force, M.P. Coy had to be alert to the varying legal codes of the national forces. Thus, for example, in cases of drunk driving, British, Canadian, and Irish soldiers could not be subjected to blood or urine tests unless permission was given; while for Danes, Finns, and Swedes, such tests were at the discretion of the investigating officer. It is interesting that an examination of M.P. Coy records revealed no nationality to have a disproportionate predilection to misbehave. But even more noteworthy, it was the general opinion of Cypriots—Greek and Turkish alike—as well as my own judgment, that the military personnel of UNFICYP displayed uncommonly high standards of soldierly conduct.

General standards. Applying equally to all United Nations soldiers and facilities in Cyprus were a set of regulations specifying uniform codes of behavior and standards. These UNFICYP regulations derived from the status-of-forces agreements and were codified in the UNFICYP standard operating procedures. The thrust behind the uniform standards was to assert as widely as possible the symbolic presence of the United Nations and to project the impartiality and neutral stance of UNFICYP. The United Nations flag was to be flown permanently on all UNFICYP premises and illuminated at night. All UNFICYP vehicles displayed UN flags in either pennant, painted, or decal form. National flags of the contingents were to be flown only by written permission from UNFICYP headquarters and were restricted to occasions such as national holidays, ceremonial parades, funeral ceremonies, and visits of national dignitaries.

The UNFICYP uniform consisted of specially issued United Nations accessories which were to be worn in conjunction with standard military dress or UN-issued olive-green shirts and trousers. Outside of their camps, whether off or on duty, all UNFICYP personnel were required to be in military uniform; mufti was permitted only off-duty and within the perimeters of the camp. The most distinguishing feature of the UNFICYP uniform was the mandatory United Nations headgear. At the discretion of the contingent commander, the official UNFICYP headdress could be either a blue beret, a blue field cap, or a blue helmet liner. In addition to the UN headgear, all UNFICYP soldiers were required to wear a blue UN sleeve emblem. The wearing of a UN scarf, also blue, was optional. To the not so casual observer, it was remarkable how a few UN accoutrements on otherwise diverse military garb could give all UNFICYP soldiers a common United Nations appearance.

Off-duty restrictions on UNFICYP soldiers were strict. After 6 P.M., soldiers leaving the camp were to be in the company of at least one other member of UNFICYP, presumably to reduce the likelihood of getting into trouble. Even more stringent, all off-duty UNFICYP soldiers of the rank equivalent to staff sergeant or below were required to be in camp before 1:00 A.M. In some cases contingent restrictions were even more severe than the UNFICYP regulations. The only exceptions to the above regulations were UNFICYP personnel whose families had accompanied them to Cyprus; practically speaking, this meant only headquarters staff officers. The vast majority of UNFICYP soldiers—officers as well as other ranks—were bachelors or had their families at home.

In order to avoid any implications adversely reflecting on the impartiality of the peacekeeping force, UNFICYP personnel were enjoined to limit their contacts with Greeks, Turks, and Cypriot nationals. An UNFICYP soldier could not accept an overnight invitation to a Greek or Turkish Cypriot household. It was also informally understood that even an invitation to a meal by either a Greek or Turkish Cypriot should be declined if possible, or at least counterbalanced by a similar invitation from the opposite ethnic community. No UNFICYP dependent could accept employment from a Greek, Turk, or Cypriot either in a governmental or commercial capacity. No UNFICYP personnel could visit or transit through Greece or Turkey. Any United Nations soldier marrying a Cypriot woman would be immediately repatriated home. The overall effect of these restrictions was to foster a code of aloof neutrality which was rigorously adhered to, in the main, by the United Nations soldiers.[8]

Social Organization: Line and Staff

The national contingents. The requirements of the overall UNFICYP regulations buttressed other commonalities throughout the peacekeeping force in Cyprus. All six national contingents were recruited from Western parliamentary democracies with advanced standards of living, and all broadly shared a common Northern European culture. From the linguistic standpoint, the contingents from Great Britain, Canada, and Ireland—which for purposes of convenience will be collectively termed the Atlantic contingents—were all native English-speakers.[9] Even among the contingents from Denmark, Finland, and Sweden—which again for convenience will be collectively designated as the Nordic contingents—there was a sizable number for whom English was a second language[10]. Thus English, which was the official language of UNFICYP, also readily served as a lingua franca between the national contingents as well. Beyond these broad cultural factors, the six contingents were also similar in being organized along the lines of reduced infantry battalions. And with the partial exception of Britcon, the contingents rotated on a six-month tour of duty in Cyprus.

There were also, however, major differences between the national contingents in their recruitment and formation. Britcon and Cancon were ongoing integral military units composed entirely of regular career soldiers. Such units as the "Pompadours" of Great Britain and the "Black Watch" of Canada were made up of men who had soldiered together before coming to Cyprus and would presumably continue to do so afterwards. Dancon, Fincon, and Swedcon, on the other hand, were formed specifically for UNFICYP duty and were demobilized after their tour—to be replaced by another ad hoc unit. Moreover, the Nordic contingents consisted, except for senior officers, of reservists who had taken a temporary break in their civilian pursuits to volunteer for UNFICYP duty. The Irish contingent followed yet another pattern. Like the other Atlantic contigents, Ircon consisted of career regular soldiers, but like the Nordic contingents it was an ad hoc volunteer unit formed specifically for a six-month tour in Cyprus.

From the perspective of their home countries' military manpower policies, the soldiers of UNFICYP could be categorized as follows. Great Britain and Canada, with no conscription, had all-volunteer armies. But if a British or Canadian soldier was a member of a unit destined for UNFICYP assignment, he could be involuntarily sent to Cyprus (or anywhere else for that matter). Thus soldiers in Britcon or Cancon were not really screened for United Nations duty. Ireland also had no conscription and likewise had an all-volunteer army. But Irish soldiers would specifically volunteer for an UNFICYP tour and hence be temporarily removed from their regular home units. Thus Ircon soldiers could be thought of as "double volunteers" in UNFICYP. Contrarily, in the Nordic nations there was a mandatory active-duty military obligation, followed by a reserve obligation, for nearly all young men. UNFICYP volunteers in the Nordic contingents were recruited from the reserve pool and, owing to a general oversubscription for Cyprus duty, could be subjected to some screening—for any disciplinary record, for presentation of self in an interview.

With such diverse recruiting systems one would expect the attitudes of the rank and file UNFICYP soldiers toward United Nations duty to vary between the national contingents. And this was in fact the case. Nearly all of Britcon's soldiers found UNFICYP duty unpleasant and tedious. Reluctant members of UNFICYP to begin with, they enjoyed no extra pay advantages and were quick to contrast their primitive living conditions with the comfortable facilities in the nearby British sovereign bases. Cancon soldiers, though not to the extent of the British, also generally found UNFICYP duty onerous. As one Canadian summed it up: "You have to make the best of it here or it's back to civie street." But some of the tedium was alleviated by two-week leaves at a special Cancon sea resort in Cyprus—an option not available to Britcon. Among the other ranks in both the British and Canadian contingents a strong-enlisted-man-cum-working-class culture seemed to foster a pervasive bad-mouthing of UNFICYP duty, though in private many of these same soldiers would acknowledge positive value in seeing Cyprus and doing something different.

The soldiers of the Nordic contingents, on the other hand, were much more favorable toward duty in Cyprus. Indeed, with some variation between contingents, between 20 and 30 percent of the Nordic volunteers were on at least their second UNFICYP tour. Mostly semiskilled workers with a sprinkling of college dropouts, the Nordic other ranks saw UNFICYP assignment as a welcome break in the civilian routine and as a chance to enjoy some sun and surf. But, most important, the extra UN pay allowances (non-taxable) could make an UNFICYP tour a relatively remunerative six months. As one man bluntly put it: "Don't you believe we're here for God, peace, or the United Nations, and those kind of things. We're here for the money, plain and simple."

The Irish, despite being regular soldiers in the mold of Britcon and Cancon, much more closely resembled the Nordic contingents in their positive attitude toward UNFICYP duty. Like the Nordic contingents, about one-quarter of Ircon men were on a multiple UNFICYP tour. One factor contributing to the favorable attitude toward UNFICYP of the Irish officers and other ranks was the military opportunity to be operational and to soldier in the field. But, as with the Nordics, the principal motivating factor of the Irish rested on the extra allowances received for UN duty. I vividly remember, after asking a tableful of Irish soldiers gathered around some beer as to why they volunteered for UNFICYP, their earnest and immediate response in unison: "Money!"

The national contingents also varied in the degree of their civilianness-militariness. The Nordic contingents, composed mainly of reservists on UNFICYP contracts, were the more civilianized, while the Atlantic contingents, whose members were all regular soldiers, reflected more traditional military forms. Especially in the "Pompadours" of Britcon and the "Black Watch" of Cancon, there was an evident pride in the military heritage of the unit, although the situation of the Black Watch was clouded by the knowledge in 1970 that the brigade was soon to be deactivated and its components distributed to other Canadian land units. In the case of the Pompadours there was a regimental tradition going back to the seventeenth century, dining silver captured from Napoleon, and a world-famous marching band.

The contrasting responses of the national contingents to the touristic attractions of the eastern Mediterranean were revealing. The soldiers of the Atlantic contingents spent all of their time on Cyprus without families, and most of that time within the confines of their camps. Dancon and Swedcon, on the other hand, had "welfare officers" whose duties included arranging charter flights to bring spouses to Cyprus for two- or three-week vacations, and organizing group excursions to Cairo and Beirut for contingent soldiers (over half of the Danish and Swedish personnel took at least one of these tourist outings during each six-month UNFICYP tour). Also, in contrast to the sharply defined military images of the British and Canadian units, the Nordic contingents of UNFICYP projected their own unique national traits as a kind of instant tradition: The smorgasbord buffets of Dancon, the sauna parties of Fincon, and Swedcon's "medal days" at Camp Carl Gustav.

Another measure of the militariness of the national contingents was in their varying proportions of officers: Dancon 13 percent, Swedcon 11 percent, Fincon 10 percent, Ircon 9 percent, Cancon 7 percent, and Britcon 5 percent. The more civilianized Nordic contingents, that is, had the highest ratio of officers to other ranks. Indeed, Dancon had proportionately two and a half times more officers than Britcon, the most traditional of the UNFICYP contingents. Concomitantly, it was very apparent that the non-commissioned officer, who played a negligible role in the Nordic contingents, was a very powerful figure in the Atlantic contingents. This role was also reflected in the strong primary-group solidarity in Britcon and Cancon. For the ad hoc Nordic contingents—although, of course, friendship bonds were made—UNFICYP service did not entail contact with longtime fellow soldiers. In Ircon, although also an ad hoc unit, the soldierly comradeship resembled that of Britcon and Cancon. This was due to the small size of the Irish Army; nearly all of the officers and most of the other ranks had known each other before UNFICYP and would continue to interact in their home army after Cyprus duty. It was also significant that Andy Capp cartoons—the epitome of masculine mateship in the English-speaking world—were widely posted throughout Britcon, Cancon, and Ircon.

UNFICYP headquarters. Where national or military traditions characterized the UNFICYP line contingents, the ambience at headquarters was definitely international and overtly engaged with peacekeeping functions. The principal duties of the headquarters staff were threefold: to direct and coordinate support for the line contingents; to mediate between Greek Cypriot and Turkish Cypriot authorities in order to alleviate intercommunal incidents; and to compile and prepare reports for United Nations headquarters in New York. With English as the official and working language, the UNFICYP headquarters, despite frequent personnel turnover, operated with reasonable efficiency and multinational good humor. An UNFICYP policy had developed in which certain staff positions would be slotted for a particular contributing nation; for example, chief of staff—Canada; chief operations officer—Denmark; chief personnel officer—Finland; chief logistics officer—Great Britain; force engineer—Ireland; UNCIVPOL liaison—Austria.

Though drawn from the contributing UNFICYP nations, the headquarters staff members were not formally associated with their respective national contingents. Unlike the set six-month rotations of the line units, the tour lengths of the thirty-eight UN staff officers varied considerably. Some served only six months, but one or two years was more typical. A few staff officers had been in Cyprus for over five years. The shorter tours characterized the British, Canadian, and Irish staff members, who were all regular officers in their home countries and seconded to temporary duty with UNFICYP. The Nordic officers consisted of both regulars and reservists, with the latter group being the long-term UNFICYP staffers. Salary arrangements generally followed the pattern of regular officers being paid by their home armies, while reserve officers, in accordance with their UNFICYP contracts, received payment from United Nations funds set aside for the Cyprus peacekeeping force.

The headquarters camp was located in a former British airfield outside Nicosia, leased to UNFICYP from the Cyprus government. As befitting a financially strained peacekeeping operation, the headquarters facilities were not prepossessing. But this was somewhat mitigated by the normally short workday: 8 A.M. to 1 P.M. Most headquarters officers, who were generally accompanied by families, rented apartments or houses from Cypriot civilians and drove to and from work in privately owned automobiles. Some unaccompanied officers, primarily in the British units attached to headquarters, and all other ranks lived in rather disheveled quarters in the headquarters camp itself.

An important integrating function for the United Nations force in Cyprus was the publication of the weekly newspaper, *Blue Beret*, under the editorship of the military public information office. Issued free to all UNFICYP soldiers, the newspaper consisted of an English frontpage reporting general UNFICYP activities, an English back page covering interunit sports competition, and six inside pages devoted to coverage of the week's events in each of the national contingents (written in the language of the contingent).[11] Owing to the rapid personnel turnover throughout UNFICYP, much of the news coverage was on the order of hail-and-farewell items. Other typical *Blue Beret* headlines were: "Thanks to UNFICYP Blood Donors," "BBC TV Team Film U.N. in Cyprus," "Ircon Wins Tug of War Competition," "UNFICYP Chapel Dedicated at Austrian Field Hospital," and "Swimmer Saved by Cancon Soldier." Profusely illustrated with photographs, the newspaper was handicapped in its informal shots by UN strictures against showing men either drinking or smoking!

The most international atmosphere thorughout all of the United Nations force in Cyprus was found in the UNFICYP Officers Club. The UNFICYP staff normally took their meals at the club, and on practically any evening a goodly international assortment of officers could be found in the club's bar and lounge. Once a month it would be the responsibility of the officers from one nationality to organize an affair in which the food, drink, and decor of their country would be featured. These "national nights" would be well attended, gathering times for UNFICYP civilians and officers from the line contingents as well as for the headquarters staff. The camaraderie of the UNFICYP Officers Club was such that most of the staff preferred its conviviality over that of the officers' mess of their own national contingents (three of which—Cancon, Dancon, and Fincon— were in nearby Nicosia).

At the level of other ranks in the headquarters, the international aura was much less evident. This simply reflected the overwhelming preponderance of British other ranks at the

UNFICYP headquarters: three-quarters of the staff itself, or nine out of ten if attached headquarters units are included. The UNFICYP Sergeants' Mess had ninety-five members, of whom only five were non-British. Three additional clubs—each with forty to fifty members, all British—derived from other ranks associations within the regular British corps system: "Wheel-Em-In" of the transportation corps, "Mercury Club" of the signals corps, and "Craftmen" of "Reme," that is, royal electricians, mechanics, and engineers. An attempt was made to set up an international club of UNFICYP corporals, but the club never really functioned. As a general proposition it could be stated that headquarters other ranks, unlike headquarters officers, rarely developed close friendships with soldiers beyond their own nationalities.

Cross-national contact. With the exception of the international headquarters and military police company, UNFICYP soldiers necessarily spent nearly all of their time within the company of their fellow compatriots. Large social affairs, however, were given by each of the national contingents during every six-month rotation period. To such affairs, an open invitation was usually extended to all UNFICYP military officers and civilian officials and their spouses, as well as to selected Cypriot and embassy dignitaries and foreign visitors. The atmosphere at these affairs—with several hundred people in attendance—was that of a rather chic internationalism combined with a military bonhomie. And, while enjoyed by the guests, these affairs involved quite considerable preparations on the part of the hosts. Hence, from at least the viewpoint of the hosts, the more preferred gatherings were the small informal parties to which several officers from other contingents were invited for a less hectic time. Owing to the small size of the island and the existence of good roadways, it was very practical for most UNFICYP officers to accept a social invitation from another contingent.

For the other ranks, formal cross-national contact within UNFICYP took the form of sports competition. UNFICYP leagues existed for soccer football and volleyball. Intercontingent matches were usually well attended by off-duty soldiers and were covered in profuse detail by the sports correspondents of the *Blue Beret*. A babble of Nordic languages and diverse English accents coming from players and spectators contributed to a festively competitive air during the playing of the game. Allowing for more intimate contact, along with some comradely drinking, were the evening dart games. These intercontingent dart games were probably the closest thing to a cross-UNFICYP institution for the lower-ranking soldiers.

Off-duty UNFICYP other ranks would often (money permitting) head toward the bright lights of Nicosia's Regina Street. Despite the potential for trouble from carousing young soldiers of different countries concentrated in a cabaret area, intercontingent friction was almost unheard-of. Cross-national contact was typically limited to light banter within the bounds of language facility. The most serious incidents were nothing more than occasional outbursts when a soldier was presented with his drinking tab or when his "whiskey girl" teased more than she delivered. If his mates could not control the matter, the problem would fall into the hands of the UNFICYP military police. Sexual opportunities for United Nations soldiers were largely confined to the whiskey girls or regular prostitutes—mostly non-Cypriots who circulate between the night spots of the eastern Mediterranean. The severe sexual code of Cypriot society—Greek and Turkish alike—effectively precluded any contact of UNFICYP soldiers with local women. Some of the more fortunate could occasionally manage a dalliance with a female European tourist. But for most UNFICYP soldiers, sex life was limited to Regina Street or abstinence.

UNFICYP in Cyprus

Cypriot leaders—whether Greek or Turkish—periodically made public statements complimentary of the United Nations force. (But this cordiality did not carry over into communications to UNFICYP headquarters arising out of charges and countercharges over intercommunal incidents.) There was also general agreement that Cypriots at all levels were favorably disposed toward the United Nations force—a view confirmed by my own impressions.

Both the calming effect on Cypriot violence of the United Nations force and the good conduct of the UNFICYP soldiers accounted for this ready acceptance by the Cypriot population.[12] Although UNFICYP was only a vague presence in the everyday life of the vast majority of Cypriots, it was also the case that United Nations military officers and civilian officials gave a dash of cosmopolitanism to certain sectors of Cypriot society: embassy affairs, governmental functions, the better shops, European cultural events, restaurants with international fare. Ironically enough for a peacekeeping force, the only caustic remarks about UNFICYP one was likely' to hear among Cypriots were imputations on the fighting qualities of the United Nations soldiers—a generalization from which the British troops were specifically exempted.[13]

If the social impact of UNFICYP on Cypriot private affairs was negligible, the same cannot be said for the economy. In the decade since the peacekeeping force came into being, an estimated (U.S.) $19 million was left each year by UNFICYP in the Cypriot economy. Little wonder that, following President Makarios's appellation, the United Nations soldiers were constantly referred to by Cypriots, almost to the point of cliché, as "our favorite tourists." As one foreign commentator put it, with perhaps a little too much asperity: "Catering to the occupying garrisons has been for decades and still is the industry that keeps Cyprus from bankruptcy. If by a wild chance Cyprus ever found itself without native or visiting warriors its natural deficit economy would become an economy of utter disaster."[14] In any event, UNFICYP expenditures were a welcome and recognized fact in Cyprus.

Finally, a full accounting of UNFICYP in Cyprus must make mention of the unanticipated ways in which it affected a small number of resident foreigners. For a few United Nations soldiers such experiences would be among the most memorable of their Cyprus tours. There was the British widow of mature years who treated all Britcon soldiers as surrogate sons and was in turn regarded as slightly dotty. Or the Goethe Institute librarian whose book circulations soared to unexpected heights as the result of the readership coming from the Austrians in the field hospital and UNCIVPOL. Or the retired Swedish film editor whose retirement home in the sun was the scene of soirees for cultivated Swedish officers. Or the French teacher from Bordeaux, employed by the evening division of the Cyprus ministry of education, who was pleased to find English-speaking Canadian officers among her students. Or the Danish wife of a Cypriot businessman who was able to extend her social circle to Dancon and introduced her Danish friends to a deeper understanding of Cyprus. And there was the Irish priest assigned to Nicosia's Roman Catholic church who was flattered to accept the companionship of other sons of Erin. Such personal vignettes were also part of the UNFICYP story.

Conflict in a Peacekeeping Force

5

The number of analytical schemes available to the researcher of formal organizations are legion. Yet, when all is said and done, approaches to the examination of concrete social organizations can be reduced, heuristically, to two major conceptual perspectives. One approach is to ascertain what the stated goals of the organization are and then to examine how much success or failure the organization has in achieving these goals. This is essentially the kind of analysis which has been applied to UNFICYP in the two preceding chapters. The second perspective is to ascertain what kinds of cleavages exist within an organization and then to examine the amount and types of conflict deriving from these cleavages. In this chapter the conflict approach is adopted as the primary frame of reference.

There is the premise here that the conflict approach can serve as an especially appropriate analytical framework to describe *all* social organizations. This does not imply that UNFICYP was a notably conflict-ridden organization, but it does mean that UNFICYP, like any social organization, had its own internal and external sources of social strain. It is by this elemental comprehension of the inherent conflict in a social structure that researchers can begin to determine the essential sociological makeup of the organization under analysis. What follows then is in no sense an exposé of UNFICYP but rather the application of a general form of social analysis to one particular formal organization.

UNFICYP Conflicts

Conflict between UNFICYP and the United Nations organization. Strain between the UNFICYP organization in Cyprus and the United Nations organization in New York was apparent on several counts. One source of dissatisfaction with the UN revolved around the lack of funds appropriated to UNFICYP military expenditures; another was the perceived hurdles in the civilian bureaucracy that had to be overcome in realizing policy recommendations and directives. What we seem to have here is the perennial complaint of military officers.

A headquarters officer: "This is the biggest penny-pinching outfit you can imagine. The UN wastes millions on foolishness, and we can't even buy a wide-angle camera. Can you imagine! For a few pennies they will jeopardize the success of the whole operation."

A headquarters officer: "New York is always fouling up. Anytime we want to do something positive we have to clear it upstairs where somebody will find a reason to turn us down. You know what the UN is? It's like two elephants screwing. Lots of noise, grunts, and groans, and shit on the ground. Then it takes twenty-four months to see what comes out."

A headquarters officer: "The Secretariat is a closed circle. It resents newcomers—especially if they are military. Once I had to deal with a UN official from New York who has been a corporal or lower in the army. He hated officers no matter what their nationality. No matter what any officer said to improve UNFICYP, we could hear him thinking, 'What does that idiot in a uniform know?' That was a complicated situation."

But the major source of contention with the UN was the restrictions placed on the UNFICYP military in the performance of its mission.

A Canadian officer: "We're sent here with our hands tied behind our backs. We're like traffic cops, we can only wave our hands. The politicians won't let us have any authority. If we could use a little muscle, this whole mess would be over in two weeks."

A *Danish officer*: "Ralph Bunche made his biggest mistake when he backed down after the Agreements were made. Since then the Cyps can push us all over the place. We should never have lost the right of complete freedom of movement. Politics overrode military considerations and pushed back the chances of ever getting peace here."

A *Finnish officer*: "An officer's first responsibility is the safety of his men. This the UN has taken away from us. Here we are nothing more than a toothless paper tiger. We are supposed to be peacekeepers. That is why they gave us these bullet-proof hats [pointing derisively to his blue beret]."

It must be added, moreover, that similar and often much more aggravated complaints about political restrictions on the perogatives of the military have persistently characterized United Nations forces.[1] Indeed, though it never occurred in UNFICYP, there have been instances of outright insubordination on the part of UN military commanders in other peacekeeping operations.[2]

Conflict between UNFICYP and home military establishments. Because of the nature of its recruiting system—men seconded and units temporarily assigned to Cyprus from their home armies—UNFICYP often found itself at odds with the military establishment of contributing nations.[3] Most of this strain centered around assignment of military personnel to the UNFICYP headquarters staff. Whether or not an officer's tour would be extended depended ultimately on decisions made in his home country's defense ministry. In one instance which came to my attention, a certain staff officer sought to extend his Cyprus tour and was encouraged to do so by UNFICYP headquarters . He was nevertheless reassigned home in the wake of a small contretemps. The aftermath was that the officer and his supporters felt that UNFICYP had not forced his case with sufficient vigor, while his home military establishment perceived UNFICYP as meddling in standard assignment practices. Needless to add, the officer's standing in his own national army was compromised, and he resigned shortly after returning home.

There was also the question as to what effects assignment to Cyprus had on the military careers of UNFICYP's serving officers. Generally speaking, officers serving six-month tours in the line contingents believed peacekeeping service would have either positive or nil effects on their military careers. In the case of the British and Canadians, of course, this service in their national contingents amounted to no more than continued assignment to their regular units. Most of the Irish and Nordic officers serving in their national contingents generally held the opinion that UN assignment had minimal consequences on their military careers, although some believed UN duty offered an opportunity to demonstrate personal capabilities in an operational force, while others felt that absence from the mainstream of military advancement at home was detrimental to their military futures. Staff officers on extended tours in UNFICYP headquarters, on the other hand, had more jaundiced views as to what UN duty did for their careers.

A Danish officer: "Well it's hard to tell what would be better for my career. Being in Cyprus probably doesn't hurt it any. But it would be better to have a company back home. No question about that. UN duty is like taking a long vacation. And if the vacation gets too long they can forget about you back home."

A Swedish officer: "Because we don't have a standing army, it is very important to be close to Stockholm to help your career. Promotions are so hard to manage that you can easily lose out when you are removed from the powers that be. Somebody gets hurt here or on the Suez Canal and they say serves him right for trying to make extra money."

The elemental fact was that UNFICYP was an anomalous military structure: an officer served in a centrally commanded international force, but the power of permanent assignment and promotion rested in his home military organization. Thus, whatever an officer's UNFICYP assignment and whatever his personal commitment toward a UN peacekeeping force might be, he knew that in both the short and long run his career advancement depended upon how he was evaluated within his own national army.

Conflict between headquarters UNFICYP and national contingents. Much of the conflict between headquarters UNFICYP and the national contingents was similar to that usually found between headquarters and line units in any military organization. There were criticisms by the national contingents that headquarters was overstaffed and overly bureaucratic, or that it failed to take the contingents into account when policies were changed. For example, when the national contingents were redeployed in the spring of 1970 (in anticipation of a forthcoming reduction in UNFICYP strength), there was contingent resentment at the need to move out of established areas and to be relocated in new surroundings.

A Danish officer: "It will be disastrous to move the contingents around. It takes years to get to know the local situation and who is who in both Greek and Turk sides. If headquarters is thinking about cutting back, the first place to start should be at headquarters. The men in the contingents are working full-time seven days a week, at headquarters they work half-days five days a week."

A Finnish officer: "The way redeployment has been handled, I think a Finn corporal could do a better job running UNFICYP. We hear stories of when we will move or where we will go. But we cannot know anything for sure. We are confused when we hear so many different stories."

Certain aspects of the conflict between headquarters and the national contingents resulted from the particular exigencies of a multinational force. The use of English as the official language necessarily placed the non-English-speaking units at occasional disadvantage. There was also the recurrent feeling at the contingent level that national interest could be slighted by headquarters.

A Danish officer: "No matter how many people we have who know English, we are still handicapped by not being native speakers. Especially because it takes us a much longer time to prepare reports. They are too particular at headquarters on correct grammatical English and spelling."

A Canadian officer: "In that report [of the 1969 Economic Committee on UNFICYP] there was no mention that Canada is paying its own way. There are a lot of Canadians at home who would be damn mad if they knew we weren't getting the credit we deserve. Why headquarters didn't bring this to their attention has bothered a lot of us. UNFICYP is a thankless job for Canada."

Another vantage point illustrates a different kind of conflict between a headquarters unit and the national contingents.

An officer in the military police company: "We have a hell of a problem trying to get cooperation from the contingents. The Irish and the British try to keep control over their own M.P.'s even though they are assigned to M. P. Coy. Another case. Just after I arrived, I had to send a Finn M.P. back to Fincon because he couldn't do the job. I mean he was lazy, mean, and dumb. To make matters worse he couldn't even say hello in English. Six months later Fincon is supposed to send us another man. They send back the same guy, only this time he's a sergeant. Now we're stuck with an absolute muck-all who outranks my good men."

Conflict between national contingents within UNFICYP. One would expect differences between the national contingents to be a major source of conflict within UNFICYP. In fact there was some such conflict, but the bulk of the intercontingent strain derived from organizational features peculiar to UNFICYP rather than hostilities between nationalities per se. Thus a former UNFICYP chief of staff writes' that, when Britcon units came under the temporary control of a Swedish commander to handle an intercommunal outbreak of violence, "rather naturally for a British company commander this was galling."[4] Other such organizational tensions were over the division of labor within UNFICYP.

A Swedish officer: "We can pull our own maintenance on our vehicles, but we must send them to Dhekelia [in the British sovereign bases]. This means the work is done slower and not as well as we could do it. But, of course, this is to give the Brits at Dhekelia a job. They have to find something for them to do. The Brits are using the UN for their own purposes."

An Austrian officer: "The report [of the 1969 Economic Committee on UNFICYP] was unfair in the way it computed costs. This made the field hospital look bad compared to the British base hospitals. The report did not mention the work the field hospital is doing on dental treatment, outpatient care, and taking care of UNCIVPOL. The chief medical officer at headquarters was a Brit and he fixed the report to make us look bad and the S.B.A.'s good. The Brits are trying to get UNFICYP to use the British hospitals and close down the field hospital."

Another organizational strain centered on the quite real differences in the pay scales of the various contingents. On this score the British in particular had cause for resentment. Alone of the national contingents, Britcon received no special UN pay allowances. Although most pronounced in Britcon, the differential in UN allowances was a source of resentment for other nationalities as well.[5] These allowances were paid for from United Nations funds and were in addition to base salaries paid for by home military establishments. The allowances were highest for the Swedes and Danes: approximately $330 U.S. monthly for officers, and $100 U.S. monthly for other ranks.

A British officer: "How do you think my men feel? A British soldier makes £10 a week, and a Swede two miles down the road makes £30 a week for doing exactly the same thing. How do I explain to my men about making the world safe for peacekeeping? They want to know why they're not getting paid what that Swede is getting paid. And I don't know what to tell them myself."

A British officer: "We had a British captain at headquarters who found that his Danish driver was earning twice as much as he was. We feel like poor relations here. Even when we go to Cancon they do the treating because they know we don't have any money."

Although it was often expressed in a humorous vein, there was also some intercontingent asperity of a more chauvinistic nature reflected in negative sterotypes acquired in Cyprus.

An Irish sergeant: "Sure we can speak English with the Canadians, but my God, they're a rowdy bunch. Nobody likes a drink and a good time more than an Irishman, but those Canadians are something else again. They get loud too early, if you get what I mean."

A Danish officer: "When we took over Xeros from the Irish, you couldn't believe the filth there was. These Irish aren't civilized. The first thing we did was kill millions of cockroaches. Millions and millions of them. We made mountains out of them and burned them. They even spoke Irish. The Irish were with those cockroaches for four years and lived together like one big family."

Genuine hostility between the nationalities, however, was rare. And in those cases where it was present, the animosity had origins long preceding UNFICYP assignment—most notably that of some Irish toward the British and a few British toward the Austrians.

An Irish officer: "We just don't talk politics with the English. It's better that way, because a lot of us couldn't control ourselves once we started talking and thinking about the old days and what's going on up North right now. It's a miracle there hasn't been a good punch-up between us yet."

An Irish officer: "Let's face facts. Anti-British feeling is ingrained in the Irish temperament. The 1916 uprising is still vivid in people's minds even if they have only heard about it from their parents or grandparents. We Irish are cursed with long memories, maybe that's because we don't have much else. Even here in Cyprus a lot of the lads can't forget what some Tommy might have done to their families not so long ago."

A British officer: "The Irish and the British have a love-hate relationship. We both attract and repel one another. We don't let our squabbles get in the way here. Some of the officers still look at the Irish as a different sort of species. But not me. After all, my wife is Irish. On second thought, maybe they are different."

A British officer: "Don't forget all the top Austrian officers were Nazis. They run the field hospital just like a stalag. One of their officers can get damn obnoxious once he gets a few drinks in him. That's when he starts complaining, 'Why can't I wear my [German] medals. I won them in honor.' It's hard to forget the war without him always reminding us."

Conflict between different components within the same nationalities. In some ways conflict within the national groups represented in UNFICYP was more noticeable than that between nationalities. Common to all contingents was a tension point introduced by the shortness of the six-month rotation cycle. Due to the brevity of a contingent's tour, there was a tendency to let matters—especially housekeeping and maintenance standards—slide. Advance detachments of about-to-arrive contingents were thus often placed in the position of having to receipt property which was not always fully accounted for or in proper condition. The conflict between departing and newly arriving units was manifest in the latter's complaint that little had been done previously to beautify the compound area or to establish adequate standard operating procedures. Each unit tended to see itself as "really the first to get things in shape." There were repeated remarks in all contingents along the lines of: "You can't imagine how bad things were here before we came over."

Another source of intracontingent tension was found only in the Scandinavian units. The contingents from Denmark, Finland, and Sweden had officer complements consisting of both reservists and career professionals. The reservists on temporary active duty were on "contract" for a specific UNFICYP tour. Their pay was equal to that of career officers of the same rank. Many of the professional officers viewed their reservist counterparts as being in Cyprus simply for a paid vacation. For their part, the reservists often saw the career officers as overly concerned with military formality and picayune discipline.

A Swedish career officer: "The reserve officer comes here on contract to make some easy money and have a good time. He cares nothing about making the army run a little better, because he is not part of it. You tell me what kind of army pays its amateurs more than its professionals."

A Swedish reserve officer: "You can write a whole book on what's wrong with the Swedish army. It is rigid and authoritarian. Men who would be failures in civilian life are on the top. It is only the reserve officer who brings initiative and common sense into a fossil system. Oh the things I've learned here! The army is run by a bunch of reactionaries who don't even have any common sense."

Three of the nations contributing military units to UNFICYP—Austria, Denmark, Sweden—also contributed civilian policemen to UNCIVPOL. The relationships between the UNCIVPOL policemen with their fellow nationals on the military side of UNFICYP was a curious blend of cordiality and calculation. Natural ties of common nationality in a foreign society were sometimes strained by questions of seniority. Seemingly petty issues of protocol and precedence could lead to uncomfortable social situations.

A Danish officer: "You quickly learn that the biggest nuisances can be your own countrymen. Sometimes we get a Danish policeman who thinks we are here to serve him. You can't let them take advantage, or else they are always intruding where they are not wanted."

An Austrian officer: "When the Austrian UNCIVPOL used to visit the field hospital, there always was the problem of who should defer to who. They don't come around much anymore."

The special situation of the British, with their large military bases on Cyprus, made for another kind of resentment. Although relations between British serving in UNFICYP and the British military in the sovereign bases was not one of conflict, the Britcon soldier was hard pressed not to contrast his position unfavorably with that of British servicemen in the sovereign bases. The latter enjoyed more lenient pass privileges, more modern living accommodations, and a much greater array of post facilities. Thus the Britcon soldier suffered a sense of relative deprivation not only in comparison with his higher-paid UNFICYP counterparts but with his more privileged fellow nationals serving in Cyprus outside the United Nations.

A British sergeant: "Kitchener lived in this very camp in the 1880s. And it hasn't changed since, except that it's more run down. Yet a few miles down the road are the most comfortable British barracks in the whole world [in the sovereign bases].
Britcon is neither fish nor fowl. The British government cuts us off because we are part of UNFICYP. The United Nations cuts us off because we are part of the British army in Cyprus."

Conflict between military personnel and civilian staff within UNFICYP. Without doubt, the most structured conflict in UNFICYP was not between or within its constituent national forces, or between different levels in the military hierarchy. Rather, the most evident strain was between UNFICYP military officers and the UN civilian staff in Cyprus. In one sense this was a restatement of the prevalent belief on the part of UNFICYP officers that the civilian staff—along with the UN in New York— was letting erroneous political considerations stand in the way of military effectiveness.

A Danish officer: "In 1967 the Dancon commander went down to an O.P. on the Green Line where a Danish soldier had been disarmed by some Turkish fighters. He went down there with an automatic weapon and waved it at the Turks. He threatened to shoot the whole bunch right there on the spot. It worked. But it got the commander into a lot of trouble with the civilians back at headquarters. They were out of their minds. But that is the kind of officer I would want to serve under. An officer's first responsibility is to look after the safety of his men. How can you bring peace if your men don't respect you? This is what the civilian mind will never understand."

An Irish officer: "A little while back there was a Finn soldier who was shot at from a Greek village. The Finns drove up their armored cars and threatened to shoot the whole village right then and there if there was another shooting. This was the only correct thing to do. Otherwise the Cyps think you're free game. You have to protect your men above all else. But the Fincon commander was in serious trouble after that. The headquarters civilians really took after him. 'No, no, no. You can't touch a hair on a Cypriot.' But I'd do the same thing."

But beyond the almost pro forma complaints of the inadequacy of the civilian support given military commanders, there were numerous other tensions between military personnel and civilian staff within UNFICYP. These tensions derived from differences in social background, organizational authority, and sociopolitical attitudes.[6] Indeed, the differentiation between the two groups made UNFICYP a kind of microcosm of the civil-military conflict long noted in independent state systems. Perhaps most apparent was the pervasive resentment of the UNFICYP officer corps toward the privileges and life-styles of the UN civilian staff.

A Finnish officer: "The civilian staff are the aristocrats of Cyprus. They live like diplomats while soldiers do all the dirty work and live in old buildings and tents. I used to believe in the United Nations and give donations to it. But not after coming here. They should give money to those soldiers on the Green Line and the O.P.'s who deserve it. Not to the high living UN civilians."

A British officer: "Just look at how a UN civilian lives and how a soldier lives. The force commander's driver is field service, and makes as much as a British colonel. It's on up the line the same way. They throw posh parties for the rest of the diplomatic corps in Cyprus. The whole diplomatic corps is in this Cyprus thing together."

Compounding the military's displeasure with the particular life-styles of the civilian staff in Cyprus, there was a generalized resentment of what was thought to be a deep-seated civilian arrogance and condescension toward military personnel. On the part of some UNFICYP serving officers, there was even an ultimate questioning of the very morality of the civilian staff in their peacekeeping role.

A Swedish officer: "Ralph Bunche—we call him 'bunk'—detests soldiers. This is true of almost all UN administrative staff including that in Cyprus. It starts from the very top. We soldiers are a different breed to them. The big problem in the UN is racism. Not the usual kind, but civilian racism against the military. But we soldiers are like women. The UN can't live with us, but they can't do without us."

A Canadian officer: "You must remember that while we change every six months, the civilians stay on and on and on. This gives them a chance to dig in. They have their lives invested in this operation. If peace comes what would they do? You know the UN types, good at languages and not much anything else. Smooth and glib, but with no place to go home to. Men between countries. They live like ambassadors. The easiest way to save money for the UN is to take away the limousines and big apartments of the UN officials here. What's keeping us here is the civilians wanting to keep this thing going and milk it for all it's worth."

The underlying resentment of many UNFICYP military officers toward the UN civilian staff took one notable form in the rather frequent, and always favorable, mentions of Major General Carl von Horn. A Swedish career officer, von Horn had an impressive background in various peacekeeping activities, including command of the UN forces in the Congo. Von Horn had subsequently written a book scathingly critical of the UN civilian leadership. By coincidence von Horn was living in retirement on Cyprus at the time of my field research. Although he was persona non grata in UN official circles—in and out of Cyprus—there were circumspect, if not subterranean, informal contacts between von Horn and some UNFICYP military officers. But the comments given below were typical of many UNFICYP officers who had never personally met von Horn.

A Finnish officer: "Soldiers are always looked upon by the civilian staff as an inevitable evil. The military is something dirty for UN officials. This is what von Horn told so well in his book. If you see him, tell him he has many secret admirers in UNFICYP. He knows how soldiers are made to feel like second-class citizens by UN officials. We have three enemies in Cyprus, you know: the Greeks, the Turks, and the UN civilians."

A British officer: "Von Horn wrote what a lot of us feel. Only we can't say so publicly. But somebody had to blow the whistle on what these UN civilians are doing to the military. Von Horn is a sort of underground hero to a lot of officers who've been in the UN."

Conflict in Military Organizations: UN Peacekeeping Forces, Multinational Commands, and National Armed Forces

A more complete assessment of the sources of conflict found in UNFICYP requires that they be evaluated in terms of whether they are unique to United Nations peacekeeping forces, whether they are characteristic of multinational commands, or whether they are general for military organizations in the main (as represented by national military establishments). This is done in the comparisons given in table 3. The structured strains noted in UNFICYP—both civil-military and intramilitary—are categorized as to whether they are (a) applicable to most or all military organizations, whether national, multinational, or UN peacekeeping forces; (b) characteristic of multinational military commands including UN peacekeeping forces; and (c) characteristically found only in UN peacekeeping forces.

Table 3. Conflict in Military Organizations: National Armed Forces, Multinational Commands, and UN Peacekeeping Forces

	Source of Conflict	
Generality of Conflict	Civil-Military Relations	Intramilitary Factors
Characteristic of most or all military organizations, whether national, multi-national, or UN peace-keeping forces	Military resentment of lack of funds appropriated for its use	Staff vs. line Reserve vs. career personnel Officer vs. other ranks
Characteristic of multi-national commands and UN peacekeeping forces		Official language other than that of some units Pay differences between national units Negative stereotypes between national units Division of labor
Characteristic of UN peacekeeping forces	Minimalist definition of military's use of force Military's perception of life-styles and attitudes of associated civilian officials	Power of assignment/ promotion residing in other than operational unit

One set of conflicts was seemingly generic to military organizations inclusive of UNFICYP. Thus in civil-military relationships there was the dissatisfaction of UNFICYP military personnel with the amount of funds and kinds of facilities allotted for military purposes by civilian authorities. On this score, certainly, neither its multinational membership nor its peacekeeping mission excluded UNFICYP from one endemic source of complaint on the part of armed forces establishments. In the UNFICYP case, moreover, the living and working conditions—but *not* pay—of UNFICYP military personnel were of a lower order than those enjoyed when the personnel were regularly assigned in their home countries. Within the military organization of UNFICYP itself, there were the astringencies between staff and line units, between reserve officers and career officers, and between officers and other ranks. These kinds of UNFICYP strains were organizationally akin to those found in virtually all armies, whether national or multinational.

On a second level, there were the conflicts typically characteristic of multinational commands of which UNFICYP was one species. These conflicts centered on intramilitary factors. There were the apparently unavoidable difficulties resulting from the official use of a language which placed about half of UNFICYP military personnel at varying degrees of disadvantage. That some negative stereotypes of other nationalities were present—whether preexisting or acquired in Cyprus—seemed likewise unavoidable. The division-of-labor squabbles between certain UNFICYP units and the British sovereign bases were in one sense unique to the Cyprus operation. But in another manner these disputes were again similar to those in multinational military establishments. More serious than any of the preceding, however, were the pay discrepancies between constituent national components. Whether due to initially higher base salaries received from home military establishments or to the system of UN allowances for Cyprus duty, the resentment of the lower toward the higher remunerated was a pervasive source of tension with UNFICYP. All of this means that many of the sources of organizational conflict noted in UNFICYP derived from its multinational composition and not from the peacekeeping mission per se.

On a third level was the set of conflicts largely peculiar to United Nations peacekeeping forces. The political restrictions placed by civilian authorities on field commanders in their use of force have often been a source of contention in civil-military relations. However, the novel nature of the peacekeeping mission —the very raison d'être of UNFICYP—placed especially heavy strains on the traditionally trained United Nations military personnel in Cyprus. Similarly, civil-military relations in national military establishments are often characterized by the military's resentment of the higher living standards and perception of civilian arrogance and condescension toward military personnel. These sore points in standard civil-military relations were especially troublesome in UNFICYP because of the smallness of the force and the resultant close interaction and observation between its military officers and civilian staff. Another conflict unique to UN peacekeeping forces was found in the relationship between UNFICYP and its contributing national military establishments. This was the structured strain resulting from the organizational separation of the power of assignment and promotion from the operational unit in which an officer served. Unlike in standard armed forces, where duty and promotion/assignment are under the same chain of command, service in UNFICYP offered no permanent assignment nor any sort of advancement through United Nations channels.

From a broader conceptual viewpoint, the conflicts between UNFICYP military officers and the United Nations can be understood as deriving from the anomalous circumstance of UNFICYP representing one of the most advanced forms of military professionalism in the service of civilian political leaders. Following the theoretical distinction made by Samuel P. Huntington, civilian control of the military can be conceived as primarily entailing one of two models—the subjective versus the objective.[7] Subjective control, characteristic of premodern military systems and ideological armies, implies the absence of any clear line between civilian and military groups or between civilian and military values. The military is an integral part of a society and embodies the dominant social forces and ideologies of that society. Objective control, which has appeared in significant degree only in some modern societies, rests on a set of norms that confine the activities of military officers to the sphere of their competence. Objective control, that is, implies a high degree of military professionalism, a sharp delimitation between civilian and military interest, and the requirement that the military be an instrument of civilian elites. Most important, the objective model presupposes that there will be disagreement between military leaders and political leaders. In point of fact, the form of civilian control over the United Nations peacekeeping forces comes close to a pure model of objective control. Paradoxically enough, the conflicts between United Nations military officers and their civilian superiors were a vivid illustration of the extreme professionalism of the United Nations officer corps.

We conclude then by reiterating a cardinal point made at the outset of this chapter. The use of a conflict framework as an interpretive device does not stigmatize UNFICYP as especially rent by strife. Indeed, the emphasis on conflict given in this chapter has distorted reality to some extent by obscuring the countervailing tendencies toward consensus also existing in UNFICYP. But it is to say that like all organizations UNFICYP was no exception in possessing external and internal sources of conflict; and it is in the comprehension of these conflicts that much of the underlying structure of UNFICYP is revealed. Moreover, many of the conflicts observed in UNFICYP are common to all military organizations, with the added tensions peculiar to multinational commands. Thus, UNFICYP, although it was a unique peacekeeping force, displayed organizational qualities with ample precedent in conventional military structures, especially those qualities deriving from the inevitable professional military conflicts with civilian superiors. Finally, and perhaps most important, if and when the United Nations is employed as a peacekeeping force in other locales and crises, most of the sources of organizational conflict found in the UNFICYP case will almost certainly be recapitulated.

Peacekeeping in the Field: The Making of a Constabulary

6

Following its initial deployment to Cyprus in 1964, UNFICYP divided the entire island into zones of responsibility, each of which was assigned to one of the national contingents. These zones and their corresponding contingents were altered over the years so that more efficient use could be made of the gradually decreasing number of United Nations troops. In 1970 the six geographical regions and their contingents were: Dancon—Nicosia West, including the Greek sector of Nicosia and the hinterland to the west and south; Fincon—Nicosia East, including the Turkish sector of Nicosia and the hinterland to the east and north; Swedcon—Famagusta Zone, roughly the eastern third of the island; Cancon—Kyrenia District, the north-central part of Cyprus; Ircon—Lefka District on the northwest coast; Britcon—Limassol Zone, the southern part of the island adjacent to the British sovereign bases.

With each contingent having responsibility for a particular zone, the field context of the line units necessarily varied. Dancon and Fincon were primarily charged with Green Line peacekeeping patrols in urban Nicosia in the center of the island. Ircon was in a rural area where some UN observation posts could be reached only by foot trail. Cancon was responsible for the Nicosia-Kyrenia convoy running through the major Turkish enclave. Britcon and Swedcon, with the largest geographical areas, were overseeing isolated villages as well as their own Green Lines in Limassol and Famagusta, the island's second and third largest cities. It was also UNFICYP policy to have two or more national elements present in instances where a strong United Nations military presence was required. Thus all contingents were required to have a reserve platoon at the ready for such an eventuality. Multinational UNFICYP military operations, however, were rare and it appears that they occurred only four times in the decade following UNFICYP's formation.

The overriding feature of peacekeeping duty, whether in isolated rural outposts or urban Green Lines, was tedium and monotony. As a general rule, however, other ranks preferred duty in the outlying countryside away from the watchful eyes of officers. The head of an observation post was usually a corporal supervising three or four other ranks. The men, normally pulling their duty in two-week stints, could work out the guard schedule among themselves. The typical United Nations observation post consisted of, in addition to the observation post itself, a small encampment with combined barracks-mess complete with field telephone, a latrine, and sometimes an outdoor shower. In the city, on the other hand, soldiers singly walked Green Lines, alternating with solitary picket duty. During each watch, which could last from two to four hours, an inspection by an officer could be anticipated. Guard stations in cities and towns would be gathering points for young Cypriot children, who were viewed by the UN soldiers as a combination of entertainment and nuisance. Inasmuch as these children seemed always to know the code names of the outposts and vehicles, they were quizzically regarded as a junior fifth column. Patrols, expecially motorized ones, were enjoyed by the troops as an opportunity to move about. But even these never usually ran into anything more exciting than attacks by stray dogs.

The duties of soldiers on the United Nations observation posts were to report, and investigate if practicable, all gunfire, digging and improvements in Cypriot fortifications, low-flying aircraft, unusual vehicle movements, and any other suspicious activities. Much lip service was given at UNFICYP official briefings to the wide leeway given the soldier in the field and to peacekeeping as a "corporals' mission." Yet there was very tight control and communications between higher UNFICYP headquarters and the field soldier. In actuality, the UNFICYP other ranks and even the lower line officers acted largely as monitors; initiative and discretionary judgment was the task of the company and contingent commanders and of UNFICYP headquarters. Any untoward incident was immediately relayed back to contingent headquarters and, if need be, up to UNFICYP headquarters.[1] As one highly placed UNFICYP headquarters officer confided: "No matter what you hear, the soldier on the outpost must be absolutely kept on a short leash. Our policy is to centralize everything. Get the responsible authorities into the act as quick as possible. No S.O.P. can cover every contingency, so we have to be doubly sure no nit at the bottom gets us into World War III."

The basic reference point for all UNFICYP peacekeeping operations was a web of "agreements," "arrangements," and "understandings" between, on the one hand, the United Nations Secretariat or UNFICYP and, on the other, Greek Cypriot and Turkish Cypriot authorities. The terminology in Cyprus as to which of these various negotiations applied to what level was not always consistent, but a convention of sorts developed along the following lines.

"Agreements" were the most formal and entailed the concurrence if not initiative of the United Nations in New York. Most of the agreements were codified in December 1965, in a series of written exchanges—never publicly released—between the United Nations Secretariat, President Makarios, and Fazil Kucuk (leader at that time of the de facto Turkish Cypriot administration). These agreements were diplomatically vague but generally laid down conditions specifying no departure from the intercommunal military status quo as of 1965 and the freedom of movement of UNFICYP units throughout the island. The latter aspect of the agreements had never been fully worked out and always remained a source of discomfort amont UNFICYP military officers. It was understood that UNFICYP units would have access to all major roads and to all other roads except those passing through Cypriot military bases. Even the restricted areas were subject to inspection by selected senior UNFICYP officers. In practice, however, UNFICYP movement throughout the island ran into frequent interferences—several times a month in 1969-70—from either Greek Cypriot or Turkish Cypriot armed elements. On the occasion of such interferences—whether planned by higher authorities or taken at the initiative of a local Cypriot armed element was not always clear—there occurred a series of negotiations and renegotiations between UNFICYP and the communal authorities. Following the protests of UNFICYP, the negotiations usually resulted in the reopening of the road to United Nations forces. Nevertheless, the constant harassment of UNFICYP units in their freedom of movement was perhaps the most galling feature of peacekeeping duty for UNFICYP military personnel.

"Arrangements" were between contingent commanders—in concurrence with UNFICYP headquarters—and Greek Cypriot and Turkish Cypriot military officials in the appropriate zones. These arrangements, which were usually written down, made more concrete the general guidelines of the agreements. The main substance of the contingent arrangements was the delineation of the status quo of Cypriot military fortifications; repair and maintenance of old positions was permissible, but extension of them or construction of new positions was not. Other matters covered in arrangements included the avenues of ingress and egress of Cypriots when approaching territory occupied by their communal opposites, the placement of UN observation posts, and—when tensions were sufficiently reduced—the closing down of observation posts.

"Understandings" were at the lowest level and were never in writing. Understandings were tacit itemizations of the monitoring standards of local UNFICYP units positioned adjacent to Greek Cypriot or Turkish Cypriot military fortifications. These understandings constituted the day-to-day surveillance duties of UN observation posts. For example, are there now four soldiers in a Cypriot Turkish outpost where formerly there had been only three; has an extra layer of sandbags been added to a particular Greek Cypriot bunker; when does maintenance (allowed) shade over into improvement (disallowed)? Such understandings existed for virtually all UN positions and were passed down from each departing unit to its replacement. And it was especially during times of contingent rotation—when understandings were most fluid—that the stalemated Cypriots were tempted to alter their tactical positions to their own advantage. But once rotation had been accomplished—with perhaps slightly bent understandings—matters usually returned to the status quo ante. For the ordinary UNFICYP soldier, then, the direct requirements of his peace-keeping duties were learned from a kind of lore tailored to each UNFICYP observation post, convoy control, road patrol, or Green Line. Rarely privy to written UNFICYP documents, the United Nations soldier received his peacekeeping instruction from his immediate supervisor, his fellow comrades, and the field situation itself.

Use of Force

If the instructions concerning UNFICYP field responsibilities were informally passed on and locally specific, the UNFICYP standards on the use of force were quite formal and centrally imposed. The minimal use of force is a cardinal tenet of UN peacekeeping forces and the root condition of the constabulary ethic. No deviation from UNFICYP regulations on the use of force was permitted, and all unit commanders were required to transmit the relevant UNFICYP guidelines to all troops in their command. Virtually every UN soldier I talked to had received such instruction and understood its terms and import.

The general conditions on the use of force were set forth in paragraph 16 of the 1964 aide-mémoire issued by Secretary-General U Thant concerning "some questions" on the operation of UNFICYP.[2] "Troops of UNFICYP shall not take the initiative in the use of armed force. The use of armed force is permissible only in self-defence. The expression 'self-defence' includes: (a) the defence of United Nations posts, premises and vehicles under armed attack; (b) the support of other personnel of UNFICYP under attack." Yet in paragraph 18 of the aide-mémoire, force was also authorized as a last resort in the event of "attempts by force to prevent [UNFICYP soldiers] from carrying out their responsibilities as ordered by their commanders." Thus, the definition of "self-defense" suddenly became more inclusive. In practical terms, this meant the notion of self-defense could be situation-specific and not limited to defense against unprovoked assault. But the criteria on the minimum use of force remained anchored on the fundamental principle of nonaggression. And there appears to have been no case in over a decade of peace-keeping deployment in which an UNFICYP soldier initiated fire. Indeed, during this same period, there seem to have been only a few instances in which an UNFICYP soldier even returned fire.

The detailed specification on the limits of force were found in the local UNFICYP Standard Operating Procedures. Inasmuch as the UNFICYP S.O.P. was the core document on the use of force, its terms deserve some explication. "Force" is generally defined as the use of physical means to impose the will of the United Nations. In order of increasing severity, force can be either unarmed, weaponed, or the opening of fire. Unarmed force is the employment of all means, other than weapons, to impose the UN's will. Examples of unarmed force include construction of barricades, manhandling, use of engineer equipment to remove obstacles, and tear-gas grenades. Weaponed force is the use of any physical instrument, military or nonmilitary, to impose the UN's will, for example, clubs, batons, rifle butts, bayonets. These lower levels of force may be used—but not necessarily—when all peaceful means of persuasion have failed. In no situation may the United Nations initiate the opening of fire. The guiding principle of the UNFICYP S.O.P. was that peacekeeping is based on preventing or stopping incidents by negotiations and persuasion rather than by the use of *any* force.

The use of firepower is to be restricted to self-defense within the latitude allowed for returning fire in the event of attack while carrying out officially commanded tasks. It is to be anticipated that commanders will not place their troops in situations where such recourse to fire will be likely. Specifically, the UNFICYP S.O.P. authorizes the opening of fire as the extreme measure of self-defense for directly endangered UNFICYP troops and for the support of other UNFICYP troops under attack. All means of warnings such as barbed wire, loud-speakers, and tear gas will be used whenever possible before fire is opened. If, despite these warnings, attacks are made endangering the physical safety of UN troops, they will defend themselves by resisting with minimum force. Should it be necessary to open fire, warning shots will be fired before resorting to aimed fire. While aimed fire will be for effect, it should be directed low, at the legs of the attackers. Firing must at all times be controlled and not indiscriminate. In all cases fire will continue only so long as necessary to achieve its immediate aim of defense. The commander on the spot will attempt to keep a record of the number of rounds fired; an endeavor will be made to collect and count empty cartridge shells after each incident.

In situations where time does not permit reference to higher authority, the UNFICYP S.O.P. continues, the commander on the spot will make the decision to use that amount of force necessary for immediate defense. Through foresight, however, commanders at all levels should anticipate dangerous situations and obtain clearance in advance from UNFICYP headquarters to use force should it be necessary. Automatic weapons or explosive projectiles can be used only if a UN position is unmistakably, deliberately, and directly attacked, and their use requires the personal authority of the force commander. In all circumstances the overriding principle of minimum force will be strictly applied.

Peacekeeping Incidents

The UNFICYP stricture on the use of force precluded the employment of the United Nations as a "third force" in the Cyprus dispute. In actual fact, in the over decade-long existence of UNFICYP, there have been few instances—less than a half dozen—in which United Nations troops were deployed in a fashion threatening the use of force.[3] By far and away the typical UNFICYP field duty revolved around managing incidents through third-party negotiations, recourse to Cypriot authorities to control their armed elements, and moral one-upmanship. Or as one long-term UNFICYP officer indelicately phrased it: "Bullshitting, bullshitting, all the time." A sense of the routine of United Nations peacekeeping can perhaps be illustrated by synopses of several incidents which occurred during the period of my field research in Cyprus. These were incidents which I had the opportunity directly to observe in their entirety, or at least to learn of their resolution through informed second-hand accounts.

In the early hours of a January evening, three shots were heard on the Nicosia Green Line. The Dancon sentry near the shooting was unable to ascertain precisely where the shots came from, but an incident report was forwarded to UNFICYP headquarters. The next afternoon the Cypriot Turkish administration lodged a strong protest with United Nations officials, charging that Greek Cypriot soldiers without provocation had fired three shots across the Green Line in the Direction of a macaroni factory where a Turkish outpost was located; ominously, the protest stated that the Turks would not be responsible for subsequent events. A Dancon team consisting of two officers and one other rank, which I accompanied, had begun to investigate the incident even before the United Nations' receipt of the Turkish protest. The investigatory procedure and relevant interrogation went as follows.

Dancon team going over to the Cypriot Turkish position and talking to the Turkish soldiers, still on duty, who claimed to be the objects of the fired shots: "Where did the shots come from last night?"

"Those drunk Greeks," pointing to the Cypriot Greek soldiers some fifty meters on the other side of the Green Line.

Dancon team crossing the Green Line and questioning the Greek Cypriot soldiers: "Did you fire any shots last night?"

"No."

"Were any of you drinking?"

"No."

"Our man here [the Danish sentry] said there was a lot of noise here last night." (This white lie was a bluff.)

"Ah, you mean our little party. Nobody was drunk."

"Well, what happened to upset the Turks?"

"Those crazy Turks, they shot at us. And we fired two shots in the air to let them know we're still here. Nothing happened."

Back to the Cypriot Turkish outpost: "Did someone here shoot across the Green Line last night?"

"No."

"Let us look at your weapons so we can count the shells."

"No."

"Do you want us to ask your superiors to count the shells?"
(Another bluff.)

Embarrased looks.

"You know accidents can happen some time. Did anyone shoot off a round last night by mistake?"

Silence. No comment.

A final report was written by Dancon in which the investigating team surmised that a Turkish Cypriot soldier had accidentally fired a shot, probably not across the Green Line. This first shot had been followed by two others from the Greek Cypriot soldiers, but these also may not have crossed the Green Line. No material evidence of a bullet hole was found in either the Greek or Turkish Cypriot positions. The incident was considered closed.

Another officially protested shooting incident emanated from the Greek side. A Greek Cypriot soldier in the Swedcon zone claimed his outpost had been fired upon—a single shot—from the Turkish side. A Swedcon investigation team unable to find substantiation—either Greek Cypriot evidence of a spent bullet or the corroboration of a nearby UN observation post—was ready to close the incident. The Greek Cypriot government, however, continued to press this seemingly minor point and lodged repeated protests with UNFICYP headquarters. The United Nations operations staff, almost in a mood of exasperation, announced they would send out an UNFICYP platoon to dig up the entire area and sift the dirt for the missing bullet. Whether such an excavatory operation would have been undertaken became moot when the Greek authorities, presumably leery of having UN troops probing all over one of their encampments, suddenly decided to drop their charges.

A third incident illustrative of everyday peacekeeping problems occurred while I was visiting a Britcon platoon stationed in a bicommunal village. The village was divided into Greek and Turkish quarters by a dry creek spanned by a small bridge. According to local arrangements, Cypriot Turkish civilians or unarmed fighters in mufti could walk across the bridge into the

Greek sector, but Cypriot Turkish fighters in uniform could not. At the same time I was there, a Turkish fighter unarmed and without cap, but otherwise in uniform, walked *under* the bridge to the Greek side and then returned the same way. Two issues were thus joined: was a Turkish fighter without his cap really not in uniform, and was walking under the bridge the same as walking on the bridge? The act of the Turkish fighter was witnessed by the Britcon soldiers, and an excited Greek Cypriot policeman brought it to the immediate attention of the platoon lieutenant. Britcon headquarters was notified, and in subsequent discussions with Turkish authorities it was agreed that walking under the bridge was equivalent to walking on the bridge. But the UNFICYP adjudication also declared that, as the Turkish fighter had his cap off and was unarmed, he was allowed the same privileges accorded Cypriot Turkish civilians. This Solomonic decision by the United Nations seemed to appease both sides.

A fourth occurrence has become widely known in UNFICYP circles as the "Hanley's Hill Incident." Informally named after a Canadian corporal, Hanley's Hill was a Cancon observation post situated in an area which had become quiet. Accordingly, Cancon abandoned the post only to see a Greek Cypriot force quickly reoccupy it in blatant disregard of the status quo arrangements. Repeated efforts by UNFICYP to persuade the Greeks to vacate the post met with failure. Finally, in a moment of inspiration the Cancon commander ordered a cesspool vehicle to fill up the surrounding trenches with feces. This caused the Greeks to remove themselves from Hanley's Hill. Nevertheless, the United Nations had to resume its occupancy of the observation post— after refilling the trenches with dirt.

A final incident to be related probably represents the absolute minimal level of peacekeeping. While spending the night with an Ircon squad manning an observation post equidistant between Greek Cypriot and Turkish Cypriot positions, we were rudely awakened by a tremendous cacophony of voices. Epithets in Greek, Turkish, and English were being hurled between the two opposing camps in great and noisy abandon. The Irish corporal in charge went out of our hut and gave forth with a loud "Shut Up!" Our nearby Greek and Turkish neighbors promptly quieted down.

Emergence of a Constabulary Ethic

The emergence of a constabulary ethic among United Nations soldiers over the course of their Cyprus tours was a very noticeable development. Behavioral adherence to the minimum-of-force concept was virtually universal and, over time, increasingly normative as well. That is, successful adaptation to the constabulatory role characterized UNFICYP soldiers whether they were civilian reservists from the Nordic countries or the regular soldiers of the Atlantic contingents. This uniformity across national lines was all the more remarkable in light of the wide divergences in military background and motivation for being in Cyprus represented by the UNFICYP soldiers. Yet the development of a constabulary ethic among UNFICYP soldiers had a paradoxical quality. On the one hand, most of the officers and men of UNFICYP displayed an ongoing redefinition of the soldierly role toward a role consistent with the absolute minimal use of force. On the other hand, the positive accomplishments of the UNFICYP peacekeeping mission—the saving of lives and the forestallment of a larger war—were rarely ever acknowledged by the other ranks of UNFICYP and not much more often by contingent line officers.

Over the course of his six-month tour in Cyprus, the UN soldier underwent definite changes in attitudes toward both the peacekeeping definition and the constabulary ethic. The characterization to be given of these attitude-shifts is based upon my extensive participant observation at various intervals in all UNFICYP units. Of course, attitude changes among UNFICYP soldiers varied depending upon individual personality and field experiences, but they typically went through three rather discrete phases.

Immediately upon arrival in Cyprus and for several weeks thereafter, the UNFICYP soldier is adjusting to his new military routine and physical surroundings, receiving formal and informal instruction on the minimum use of force, and becoming acquainted with the operative arrangements and understandings applying to his particular assignment. He carries into the initial period a preconceived and somewhat idealized norm of peacekeeping, which is that of imposing quick and final solutions on the Cyprus embroglio. The propensity in the first phase is to think of peacekeeping in "third force" terms that foster an activist definition of the soldier's role—an arbiter rather than a negotiator of peace. In point of fact when United Nations soldiers were first exposed to the UNFICYP regulations on minimal force, their reactions ranged from dutiful compliance to outright disbelief.

The initial period gives way to a second phase, lasting a month or two, in which the soldier's attitudes take certain seemingly paradoxical turns. The earlier idealized and activist definition of peacekeeping is replaced by an opposite cynicism. Frequent sentiments are heard along the lines of the futility of letting the "Cyps run all over you," or of how the Cypriots prolong the United Nations presence for their own economic advantage. But the disillusionment with peacekeeping does *not* work against a constabulary ethic per se. Quite the contrary, the cumulative impact of the field experience seems to engender a normative commitment to minimal force standards which corresponds with the always present behavioral adherence to the constabulary role. Longitudinal analysis of UNFICYP soldiers, that is, indicates an inverse correlation between positive evaluation of peacekeeping and the emergence of a constabulary ethic. Put in another way, cycicism with peacekeeping comes to predominate among UN soldiers at the same time that restraint in force becomes routinely acceptable.

The third and final phase of the Cyprus tour finds yet another conjunction of attitude sets among United Nations soldiers. The mood of peacekeeping cynicism gives way—though not consistently—to a realistic but somewhat positive evaluation. Representative of the peacekeeping reevaluation were statements such as, "I used to knock UNFICYP a lot, but I know now that we have stopped a lot of killing, and that's no small thing." And "Sure UNFICYP isn't much, but at least we've kept the Greeks and Turks from each other's throats." Such reassessments of UNFICYP were more characteristic of UNFICYP officers and other ranks beyond a first tour. But as their time in Cyprus came to a close, there was a discernible trend even among single-tour UNFICYP soldiers to evaluate peacekeeping in limited yet favorable terms. Concurrent with the more realistic appraisal of the peacekeeping mission, the constabulary ethic became even more pronounced.

The modal reaction of the United Nations soldier toward the latter part of his tour was one of quizzical tolerance of the perceived antics of the Cyprus disputants coupled with a reluctance to use force even if hypothetically so ordered. On numerous occasions I heard UN soldiers on duty wonder aloud if they would fire upon a Cypriot—barring self-defense—no matter what the provocation. By the time they left the island, most UNFICYP soldiers appeared to have consciously absorbed the constabulary ethic while possessing mixed views toward the efficacy of the peacekeping enterprise.

This anomaly—the linkage of an emergent constabulary ethic with a contradictory attitude toward United Nations peacekeeping —is one of the most important findings to arise out of the research reported in this study. And while grounded in participant observations, this finding is further corroborated by interview data which will be documented in following chapters. For present purposes, however, it is important to stress the generalization that the constabulary ethic was primarily engendered by on-duty, in-the-field peacekeeping experiences. This is also to say that informal learning arising out of the field situation was a more determining factor in forging the constabulary ethic than was peacekeeping training prior to arrival in Cyprus. Indeed, what is striking is how the constabulary ethic developed so uniformly among all UNFICYP troops despite the major differences between the various national contingents in their military organization and prior peacekeeping training.

An approximate rank ordering of the specialized peacekeeping training given to each of the national units prior to arrival in Cyprus would in descending order be: Cancon, Swedcon, Dancon, Fincon, Ircon, and Britcon. The first three national contingents, especially, formed a group in which peacekeeping training was relatively intensive; a month for the ad hoc Swedish and Danish units, and even longer in the regular army contingents of the Canadians. Such peacekeeping training included new or refresher courses in crowd control, road blocks, use of batons and shields, mounting guards and pickets, protection against mines and booby traps, hygiene, sanitation, and first aid. Additionally, special indoctrination was given on the United Nations,

Cyprus, and peacekeeping in general. Fincon and Ircon assembled two or three weeks before going to Cyprus, and the predeployment period was devoted to housekeeping duties, weapons distribution, medical processing, and a cursory area introduction to Cyprus. Britcon received little if any peacekeeping training or indoctrination and operated on the assumption that a conventionally well-trained soldier under proper leaership would be flexible enough to perform peacekeeping duties.

Yet, and this generatization must be reiterated, there were few if any observable differences among the national contingents in the behavioral adaptation to the constabulary role, and few differences, therefore that could be attributed to prior peacekeeping training. This uniform adherence to the minimum-of-force concept also occurred despite the previously noted attitudinal differences between the national cotingents: The British and Canadian soldiers—all members of integral units ordered to Cyprus—were generally resentful of their UNFICYP assignments, while the Irish and Nordics—all UNFICYP volunteers—typically valued the peacekeeping assignment for its monetary and travel benefits. Again we return to the finding that field experiences were the prime determining factor in accounting for the emergence of the constabulary ethic among UNFICYP soldiers.

The national units, however, were distinguishable in their cognitive knowledge of Cyprus. This was revealed by an informal poll taken of several score other ranks in each of the contingents. Soldiers were asked, whenever the opportunity arose, a question (sometimes through interpreters) which presumably measured at least a superficial familiarity with Cypriot society; namely, did they know whether there were more Greeks or Turks on the island. The differing responses to this question between the Atlantic and Nordic contingents were glaring. Upwards of three-quarters of the Swedes, Danes, and Finns knew there were more Greeks than Turks on Cyprus, while less than a quarter of the Canadians, Irish, and British were as well informed. Some of the more resourceful responses of the Atlantic soldiers went as follows. An Irish private: "Well, whatever it is, there are too damn many of them." A Canadian corporal: "There are three kinds of Cyps: Greek Cyps, Turk Cyps, and Cyp Cyps. The last bunch is the biggest and they're the ones who don't give a damn.'' (Perhaps unwittingly, this soldier was closer to the truth than I first suspected.)

There are several points to be made about the results of this informal survey of United Nations other ranks. (Officers of all contingents were, as one would expect, more sophisticated and possessed at least a minimal knowledge of the broader peace-keeping mission and the general social statistics of the Cyprus population.) Initially, it is apparent that the amount of prior peacekeeping training and area indoctrination does not seem to explain cognitive understanding of the demographic-cum-political context of the peacekeeping mission. Thus the Canadian other ranks, despite their intensive introduction to Cyprus, differed little from their British and Irish counterparts in their low level of knowledge about Cypriot society. Inversely, the Finn other ranks, recipients of relatively little prior exposure to Cyprus facts, shared the same high cognitive levels of their Nordic counterparts who did have prior area indoctrination. A plausible explanation of the differential awareness of the local scene is that the civilian reservists who made up the Nordic contingents appeared to be drawn more from the lower middle-class of their home countries as compared to the more typically working-class soldiers of the Atlantic contingents. And this relative social advantage—with attendant higher education—served to predispose the Nordics toward more curiosity and receptiveness to what the situation in Cyprus was all about. Moreover, it is noteworthy that even after several months or more of peacekeeping in Cyprus, most Atlantic other ranks were still oblivious to the island's basic demographic realities. When left to themselves, there was a remarkable disinclination among the soldiers of the Atlantic contingents to engage in talk about either the peacekeeping mission or Cyprus itself. Grossly erroneous remarks on Cypriot society were rarely countered by corrective information. But in the Nordic contingents there was a touristic inquisitiveness which led to some exchanges on where to go, what to see, and how people lived in Cyprus.[4]

Perhaps the most important observation on the cognitive variability concerning Cyprus of the UNFICYP soldiers is that such cognition operated independently of the peacekeeping performance. For, despite the sharp differences between the Atlantic and Nordic contingents on their knowledge of Cyprus, there was nevertheless a cross-contingent uniformity in the display of minimum-of-force standards and impartial behavior. This is not to say that occasional sentiments indicating more sympathy with one side over the other were never privately expressed. Generally speaking, there was a slight disposition among many UNFICYP soldiers to sympathize with the Turkish Cypriots, who were seen as underdogs. There was also a somewhat more favorable stereotyping of the Turkish Cypriots, who, compared to the Greek Cypriots, were viewed as more open, more honest, more generous, and less ingenious. But, and this point must be heavily underscored, the vague sentimental sympathy for the Cypriot Turks never took the form of prejudicial behavior. By far, the dominant mood among UNFICYP soldiers toward Cypriots was that of "a plague on both your houses."[5] Moreover, the proclivity of both Cypriot communities to take whatever petty tactical advantage they could of UNFICYP strengthened the canon of impartiality.[6] While this can only be conjecture, it is possible that had one or the other of the two communities unilaterally desisted from pressing a forward strategy vis-à-vis UNFICYP, the impartial stance of the United Nations peacekeepers might have been subject to some erosion.

Peacekeeping, Internationalism, and the Constabulary Ethic

7

The collection of data for this study of United Nations peace soldiers was obtained by a variety of methods. Much of the information was derived from analyses of peacekeeping documents and field observations and has already been presented. Additionally, however, information was collected in formal interviews with 110 UNFICYP officers—slightly under one-third of the total UNFICYP officer complement. With some minor deviations, the 110 interviewed officers were selected so as to create a representative cross-section of the UNFICYP officer corps in terms of nationality proportions and unit assignments. Moreover, although the interviews fell at different times of the officers' stays in Cyprus, an effort was made to conduct interviews as late as practicable during the UNFICYP tour. Inasmuch as most of the questions asked in the interview schedule were of the open-ended variety, the tabular data to be presented derive from my own categorization and grouping of the interview responses. It is believed, however, that in almost all cases—because of the directness of both the questions and answers—there was little ambiguity in coding the responses into relatively discrete attitudinal categories.

Social and Political Values

The dominant attitude set of the UNFICYP officer corps was one of political and social conservatism. One question asked of the

officers was: "On political matters at home, with whom would
you say you generally agree—the left, the right, or the center?"
As given in table 4, 67 percent of the officers characterized
themselves as politically to the right, 27 percent were most
comfortable with the center, and only 6 percent regarded themselves as being on the left. Even the small number of self-
identified leftists, it should be made clear, had as their referent
social democracy rather than any forms of radical ideology. When

Table 4. Social and Political Values of UNFICYP Officers by Nationality
Groups (Percentages)

	Total UNFICYP (N = 110)	Atlantic Nations (N = 58)	Nordic Nations (N = 52)
Self-categorization of general political values			
Left	7	2	11
Center	27	26	29
Right	67	72	60
Total	100	100	100
Evaluation of recent changes in social and moral values of home country			
For the better	8	7	10
No change	27	29	31
For the worse	65	64	59
Total	100	100	100
Perception of civilian regard for military in home country			
Favorable	6	7	6
Mixed	30	29	31
Unfavorable	64	64	63
Total	100	100	100
Characterization of home country's motivation to participate in UNFICYP			
Idealistic or altruistic	5	5	4
Mixed motives	37	35	40
National interest or cynical	58	60	56
Total	100	100	100

comparing officers from Great Britain, Canada, and Ireland with those from Denmark, Finland, and Sweden, we find the Nordic officers to be only marginally less conservative than their Atlantic counterparts. And the slight tendency toward less conservatism among the Nordic officers was almost exclusively found among the reservists rather than the regular officers. But even taking this into account, the paramount finding remains that the political similarities across the nationality groupings were much more striking than the differences. It is relevant to note, furthermore, that this finding of political conservatism among UNFICYP officers parallels that of other researchers who have probed the political attitudes of military officers from Western parliamentary democracies.[1]

An item seeking to measure social conservatism was derived from the question: "Do you think there have been major changes in the social life and morals of your country in recent years? If so, do you think these changes have been for the better or worse, or does it make any difference to you?" In responses almost exactly paralleling the previous question on political attitudes, 65 percent of the officers stated social and moral values had changed for the worse, 27 percent either detected no major changes or felt indifferent about any changes, and only 8 percent thought social and moral values had changed for the better. Differences between the Atlantic and Nordic officers on this item were barely perceptible.

Some of the flavor of the prevailing political and social conservatism of the UNFICYP officers is reflected in the following statements.

A British officer: "Soldiers can't have politics. That's why they have to be right of center at all times. It's only when you are left that you are political."

A Canadian officer: "If I had to live under a dictatorship, there is no question that I would prefer a right-wing dictatorship. In left-wing dictatorship you have absolutely no chance at all. But this is something the left-wing intellectuals will never understand."

An Irish officer: "Man in travail, that's man's fate. All socialist hopes are utopian and futile. We must find whatever purpose there is in life in family, Church, and Irish identity.''

A Swedish officer: ''You can't believe what is happening to our young people. Sex and no work. Half the population works and the other half lives off the working half. Where will it end?''

A Danish officer: ''The reason we have so many troubles today is because of you sociologists. A man commits a crime and you make the judge set him free and put the policeman in jail.''

Perceptions of civil-military relations are one important element of sociopolitical attitudes. Accordingly, the UNFICYP officers were queried: ''What do you think is the general attitude of the civilian population in your country toward the army and military life in general?'' As reported in table 4, 64 percent believed that citizenry held unfavorable attitudes toward the military; 27 percent stated the public's evaluation was mixed; and only 6 percent thought the military was held in high regard. The distribution of responses to this item was virtually identical whether looking at officers from the Atlantic or Nordic countries. Here we also seem to find corroboration of a generally noted phenomenon—at least as perceived by professional military officers—of a contemporary decline in the status of armed forces in Western parliamentary democracies.[2]

Typical responses of the UNFICYP officers on the standing of their armies in their home countries are given below.

A Nordic officer: ''I've raised my son on conservative principles. But with the attitude toward the military that exists in my country, I told him not to become a professional soldier. He's in cadet school anyway. I guess he's like his father and too stubborn to go along with the new styles.''

A Finnish officer: ''I'm sorry to say that we are beginning to get them too—the bearded pacifists and hippies. How long this will go on, God knows.''

A Danish officer: ''Danish people are against the army. But wait until the enemy is at the borders, and then see how much they want us. They don't realize that we serve in peacetime to prevent war.''

A British officer: ''Rudyard Kipling said it well. Tommy this, and Tommy that. The soldier's plight is to put up with snobbery until his life is put on the line. Times don't change much, do they?''

An especially revealing aspect of the value framework of the UNFICYP officers was their assessment of the motivation for the participation of their home countries in United Nations peacekeeping operations. Specifically, all the interviewed officers were asked: "Why do you think your country decided to take part in UNFICYP?" As reported in table 4, 58 percent of the officers explained their country's participation in frankly cynical or national self-interest terms. This contrasted with only 5 percent of the officers who ascribed motives to their country which were fundamentally idealistic or altruistic, that is prevention of war, restoration of peace to Cyprus, service to the United Nations. Slightly over a third, 37 percent, characterized their country's motivation in mixed terms, mentioning both cynical and idealistic reasons. Again, the differences between the Atlantic and Nordic responses were perceptible. What is striking is that the successful behavioral adaptation to the peacekeeping role in the field occurred in the face of a widespread cynicism toward home national decisions which resulted in deployment of peacekeeping forces. No judgment is implied here as to the veracity of the officers' perceptions of their home political establishment's nonaltruistic motivations. Our concern, rather, is with how these attitudes constituted part of a prevailing political conservatism and attendant cynicism among the UNFICYP officer corps.

A representative sampling of the UNFICYP's officers' characterization of their home country's decision to take part in United Nations peacekeeping is as follows.

A Canadian officer: ''Canada takes part in United Nations peacekeeping because Lester Pearson wanted to win a Nobel Prize.''

An Austrian officer: ''We're here so Cyprus can make money off of us. The United Nations is one way the poor countries can suck off the richer ones. This is why the UN is here [rubs fingers in money-making gesture].''

A Finnish officer: ''It is to Finland's selfish interest to prevent

wars. Any trouble spot can flare into a world war which will bring
Finland right into the middle of it. What serves the noble
purposes of the UN also serves the selfish purpose of our national
interest."

A *Swedish officer:* "Sweden asks to take part in peacekeeping
because it gives us a chance to have units in the field without
costing much money. And it helps the impression of being a
world power without actually being accused of imperialism. So we
can be hypocrites—take part in international affairs while calling
others imperialists."

A *Canadian officer:* "You know why Canada is in UNFICYP.
It's the old story—when you have trouble at home, distract
attention overseas. Peacekeeping is to keep attention off Quebec.
And besides, peacekeeping is good politics. Canada can't be a
major power on its own, and peacekeeping is one way to have a
large international voice."

A *British officer:* "We're in UNFICYP for a very simple
reason. It gives us a good excuse to provide security for our
sovereign bases on Cyprus."

A *Danish officer:* "Denmark is in UNFICYP because it is
always telling other countries how to mind their business. We are
the greatest do-gooders in the world—we and the Swedes.
Denmark has the belief that it can set the rest of the world's
troubles right. We are tremendously egotistical about how much
we know. Like trying to bring down the Greek junta, or stop the
Americans in Vietnam."

An *Irish officer:* "UN duty is looked upon very favorably by
the Irish Army. It gives us a purpose and boosts our prestige at
home. When those Irish soldiers were killed in the Congo, it was
national mourning. Another fact is that UN pay gives soldiers
more money and this directly increases our prestige at home. The
more money we make, the more prestige we have. Simple as
that."

Peacekeeping Attitudes

The constabulary ethic. The emergence of a constabulary ethic
among UNFICYP soldiers over the course of their peacekeeping

tour was one of the most significant findings to arise out of the field research. To complement these behavioral observations, it was also sought to ascertain the attitudinal commitment to the constabulary ethic from the interview data. The difficulties in attempting to operationalize in questionnaire form a concept like the constabulary ethic—the minimal use of force shading into noncoercion—are severe. Nevertheless, a measure of the constabulary ethic was constructed from responses to two items: (a) "Does an officer who is well trained in military skills and who has broad leadership experience in his home army still require additional skills for peacekeeping service?"; and (b) "Can a soldier be effective in the peacekeeping job if he cannot use force except in self-defense?" UNFICYP military officers who gave affirmative answers to both questions were categorized as constabulary. All others were labeled nonconstabulary, making for a dichotomous breakdown.

As presented in table 5, the UNFICYP officer corps divided into almost equal proportions of constabulary and nonconstabulary responses: 51 percent and 49 percent. When nationality group is held constant, only slight differences appear; the Nordic officers are marginally more likely to give constabulary responses than their Atlantic counterparts. Somewhat more perceptible is the contrast between officers of the international headquarters staff with those of the national line contingents. Thus, 58 percent

Table 5. Constabulary Ethic of UNFICYP Officers by Nationality Groups and Unit Assignment (Percentages)

	Constabulary	Non-constabulary	Total	(N)
Nationality Groups				
Atlantic nations	48	52	100	(58)
Nordic nations	54	46	100	(52)
Unit Assignment				
Headquarters units	58	42	100	(24)
Line contingents	49	51	100	(86)
Total UNFICYP Sample	51	49	100	(110)

of the officers serving in the headquarters units gave constabulary responses compared with 49 percent of the line officers. The overriding finding, nevertheless, is the absence of sharp differences in constabulary responses when the sample is broken down into either nationality backgrounds or unit assignments.

Among the constabulary responses, comments as to the novel demands of the peacekeeping soldier fell into three broad categories: (a) the actual requirements of the constabulary ethic in resocializing both officers and other ranks not to use force; (b) the morale problems, especially for other ranks, associated with boredom and tedium in peacekeeping duties; and (c) the necessity to disabuse officers, especially, from notions that peacekeeping duties would result in visible and positive outcomes. Nonconstabulary responses, on the other hand, were more internally consistent and took the line that peacekeeping duty was only a change in degree and not in kind from the traditional tasks of the soldier, or even that an element of force, however masked, could serve the cause of peacekeeping. Whether giving constabulary or nonconstabulary responses, however, almost all of the interviewed UNFICYP officers raised the issue of reconciling soldierly honor with peacekeeping performance, a topic which will be returned to in a later discussion.

Internationalism. There is a strong presumption—both descriptively and normatively—in much of the extant peacekeeping literature that internationalism is a necessary factor in the successful performance of peacekeeping forces. Such internationalism ought to involve not only formal cooperation between national contingents serving under a United Nations command, but—and more theoretically important—a subjective commitment to supranational loyalties on the part of peacekeeping soldiers. For our purposes internationalism is generically considered to be a "commitment to use and be bound by political institutions transcending the nation-state."[3] Indeed, one could array nationalism-internationalism attitudes on a continuum ranging from giving no preference whatsoever to international bodies through meeting limited international obligations or preference for a stronger United Nations to support for a one-world government. More directly, our concern here is with the perceived effect of United Nations peacekeeping service on attitudes toward internationalism held by UNFICYP officers.

All the interviewed UNFICYP officers were asked: "Has serving with UNFICYP changed any of your ideas about the need for a stronger United Nations or perhaps even a form of world govenment?"[4] Their responses are summarized in table 6. United Nations military service did *not* increase internationalist sentiments. Quite the contrary. Thus, 38 percent of the officers asserted they had become less internationalist since assignment to UNFICYP, compared to 23 percent who had become more internationalist. Thirty-nine percent stated their attitudes had not changed toward becoming either more or less internationalist. The negative effect of UNFICYP service on the internationalist attitudes of the military officers is a significant finding, especially in light of much of the conventional peace wisdom which regards participation in world bodies as fostering internationalist sentiments.

Table 6. Internationalism of UNFICYP Officers by Nationality Groups and Unit Assignment (Percentages)

	More Inter- nationalist	No Change	Less Inter- nationalist	Total	(N)
Nationality Groups					
Atlantic nations	24	31	45	100	(58)
Nordic nations	23	48	29	100	(52)
Unit Assignment					
Headquarters units	46	25	29	100	(24)
Line contingents	16	43	41	100	(86)
Total UNFICYP Sample	23	39	38	100	(110)

When comparing nationality groups among the UNFICYP officers, however, some noteworthy differences do appear. Thus, 45 percent of the Atlantic officers responded that they had become less internationalist since being in UNFICYP, compared with 29 percent of the Nordic officers. From a detailed breakdown of the interview data, much of this difference seems explainable by the greater propensity of Nordic reservists to evaluate favorably the United Nations when compared with the regular officers of the Nordic contingents. Regular officers, that is, whether from Nordic or Atlantic contingents, were similar in their shared attribution of lessened internationalism following UNFICYP assignment. (It is to be remembered that all officers were regulars in Britcon, Cancon, and Ircon.) Even more sharp are the differences between the headquarters units and the national contingents. Proportionately, three times as many headquarters officers stated they had become more internationalist than the contingent officers: 46 to 16 percent. The "deviant" phenomenon of heightened internationalism among certain United Nations officers deserves special comment and will be specifically examined in the analytical framework of the next chapter.

The constabulary ethic and internationalism. Although the two variables of constabulary ethic and internationalism have been intentionally treated as discrete items in the presentation of the data given here, the two variables are almost always related in tandem in the peacekeeping literature. Moreover, as has already been discussed in our earlier review of the literature, a constant in the writing on this topic is the assumption of a peacekeeping "positive manifold," that is, the constabulary ethic and internationalism are like components and go up together. We can now turn, then, to the data given in table 7 that report the interrelationships between the constabulary ethic and internationalism based on the 110 interviewed United Nations military officers.[5]

The interview data given in table 7 show only the weakest relationship in the expected direction. Thus, 27 percent of the constabulary respondents stated they also had become more internationalist, compared with 19 percent of the nonconstabularies who had similarly become more internationalist. But when looking at those who said they had become less internationalist following UNFICYP assignment, the difference narrows to practically nothing: 37 percent of the constabularies compared to 38 percent of the nonconstabularies. There is no need to belabor the point, but the proposition that internationalism and subscription to noncoercive practices are intimately related and part of an underlying common factor is not supported by the available data. Rather, it is more accurate to regard a commitment to supra-national loyalties and constabulary notions as quite separate and independently generated phenomena. Among the UNFICYP officer corps, at least, one could find many disillusioned ex-internationalists who displayed constabulary sentiments and others who were skeptical of the efficacy of minimal force but who nevertheless developed favorable attitudes toward United Nations prerogatives.

Table 7. Internationalism of UNFICYP Officers by Constabulary Ethic (Percentages)

	More Inter-nationalist	No Change	Less Inter-nationalist	Total	(N)
Constabulary	27	36	37	100	(56)
Nonconstabulary	19	43	38	100	(54)

Peacekeeping evaluation. In addition to the constabulary ethic and internationalism, a third core peacekeeping variable was identified in evaluations of the United Nations peacekeeping operation in Cyprus. This was an effort to gauge how UNFICYP officers viewed the performance of a peacekeeping force with which they were intimately familiar. Such evaluations, moreover, were assumed to be not so indirect indicators of the officer's judgment of the worthwhileness of his own United Nations service. The measure of the evaluation of a concrete peacekeeping enterprise was taken from the single question: "Generally speaking, how successful an operation has UNFICYP been?" The standards of success were left to the determination of the respondent.

The responses to this open-ended question fell into three categories. One set of responses consisted of those who said

UNFICYP was *largely successful*. Here statements were made that UNFICYP had not only stopped the killing or prevented a larger war but had also made progress toward resolving the underlying problems of Cypriot communal divisiveness. Moreover, it was asserted that UNFICYP was a model of international cooperation and applied constabulary practices. A second category was made up of responses which viewed UNFICYP as *somewhat successful*. That is, the stopping of the intercommunal violence and prevention of war were deemed sufficiently worthwhile in their own right, despite the elusiveness of a political solution in Cyprus. Persons in this category usually offered mixed evaluations as to the operational efficiency of the United Nations force. The final category were those who saw UNFICYP as essentially a *failure*. Nothing fundamental had been accomplished, and the lessons of UNFICYP were that peacekeeping at best ought to be only a short interim operation. Some in this third group would go as far as to argue that it would be more appropriate to let the disputants fight it out among themselves and come to an accord based on local or regional power realities.

Given in table 8 are the peacekeeping evaluations of the UNFICYP officers by selected breakdowns. For the total sample, 16 percent evaluated UNFICYP largely successful, 57 percent somewhat successful, and 27 percent regarded UNFICYP as essentially a failure. When nationality groups are compared, there is some tendency for the officers from the Atlantic countries to be more negative toward UNFICYP than Nordic officers. A closer breakdown of this finding revealed that it was the Canadians among the national contingents who disproportionately accounted for unfavorable judgments of UNFICYP. This appeared to be a result of the fact that the Cancon unit at the time of the research had been in Cyprus several years earlier and many of its officers could see little change in accomplishing peacekeeping goals over the intervening time. But if one excludes the Canadians, there were only very minor differences between the contingents as to their evaluations of UNFICYP.

If the differences on UNFICYP evaluations between the nationalities were not all that pronounced, this was not the case when comparing the headquarters units with the line contingents.

Forty-one percent of the headquarters officers, compared to 9 percent of the contingent officers, termed UNFICYP as largely successful. Conversely, only 12 percent of the headquarters officers, contrasted with 30 percent of the contingent officers, regarded UNFICYP as a failure. It appears that unit assignment much more than nationality explains differences in judgments of UNFICYP's efficacy. Thus, it was the most internationalist officers—the headquarters staff—who were also most likely to evaluate favorably their peacekeeping service.

In fact, when attitudes toward internationalism are examined for their relationship with peacekeeping evaluations, the findings become very pronounced indeed. The interview data are quite clear in demonstrating a close association between heightened internationalism with favorable UNFICYP evaluations and lessened internationalism with negative opinions of UNFICYP.

Table 8. Cyprus Peacekeeping Evaluations of UNFICYP Officers by Selected Variables (Percentages)

	Largely Successful	Somewhat Successful	Failure	Total	(N)
Nationality Groups					
Atlantic nations	15	52	33	100	(58)
Nordic nations	17	63	20	100	(52)
Unit Assignment					
Headquarters units	41	47	12	100	(24)
Line contingents	9	61	30	100	(86)
Changes in Inter-nationalism					
More inter-nationalist	52	48	–	100	(25)
No change	11	66	23	100	(43)
Less inter-nationalist	–	55	45	100	(42)
Constabulary Ethic					
Constabulary	25	62	13	100	(56)
Nonconstabulary	7	55	38	100	(54)
Total UNFICYP Sample	16	57	27	100	(110)

Thus, among those who became more internationalist following UNFICYP assignment, 52 percent judged UNFICYP to be largely successful, 48 percent termed UNFICYP somewhat successful, and none regarded United Nations peacekeeping in Cyprus a failure. Contrarily, for the officers who had become less internationalist, none evaluated UNFICYP as largely successful, 55 percent saw UNFICYP as somewhat successful, and 45 percent said UNFICYP was essentially a failure. Those who were intermediate between the more and less internationalist positions gave correspondingly intermediate evaluations of UNFICYP.

The remaining relationship presented in table 8 is that between the constabulary ethic and evaluations of the United Nations peacekeeping operation in Cyprus. There is a tendency, though not marked as with internationalism, for constabulary responses to be associated with positive evaluations of UNFICYP. We find that 25 percent of the constabularies compared to 7 percent of the nonconstabularies viewed UNFICYP as largely successful. Judging UNFICYP a failure characterized 13 percent of the constabularies and 38 percent of the nonconstabularies. But it is also important to note that UNFICYP was termed somewhat successful by a clear majority of both constabularies and nonconstabularies: 62 percent and 55 percent.

In summary, UNFICYP was judged by the large majority of its serving officers to be at least partially successful in the attainment of its peacekeeping goals. But a sizable fraction—about one-quarter—of the UNFICYP officers viewed the United Nations effort in Cyprus almost exclusively in negative terms. The interview data also supported the generalization that social organizational factors—assignment to the headquarters staff or to a line contingent—accounted for more variance than cultural consideration—nationality background. The attitudinal intermesh between key peacekeeping variables, moreover, was clarified to some extent, though not always in directions anticipated in the extant literature. Most especially, the constabulary ethic and internationalism were each found to be much more closely associated with evaluations of peacekeeping success than they were with each other. In fact, the association between redefinitions of the soldierly role toward constabulary standards and heightened internationalism was tenuous at best.

But more important, the attitudinal traits of the UNFICYP officers derived from conventional interviews are to be seen in the context of the behavioral observations made in the field. It is to be reiterated that in their on-duty peacekeeping performance the soldiers of UNFICYP displayed nearly universal adherence to impartiality and absolute minimum-force practices. Moreover, it is eminently desirable that analyses of attitudinal configurations attempt to uncover processes of attitude formation *in situ*. In this regard the three core peacekeeping variables—constabulary ethic, internationalism, and peacekeeping evaluations—were subjected to analysis over time in the form of repeated interviews with a select group of UNFICYP officers. The findings from these panel interviews will be presented in the next chapter. It suffices to say at this point that the dynamics of attitude change among serving peace soldiers is a key consideration in the sociology of a United Nations military force.

The British in UNFICYP: A Special Case?

We close this chapter that presents UNFICYP interview data with a coda on the special case of the British officers participating in the United Nations peacekeeping force. For the reasons covered in the discussion of the formation of UNFICYP, British military units preceded the United Nations in Cyprus peacekeeping and in turn became integral components of the succeeding United Nations command. Indeed, throughout UNFICYP's existence British military contributions have played a most important role in the peacekeeping force both in number of soldiers and logistical backup. This unique set of occurrences has been the only exception to the peacekeeping rule that Security Council members are excluded from participation in United Nations peacekeeping forces.

From the standpoint of research in the military sociology of peacekeeping forces, the presence of the British in UNFICYP offered an exceptional opportunity to assess the peacekeeping traits of the soldiers of a major power. For it will be remembered that an accepted premise of much of the peacekeeping literature is that soldiers from major powers are inappropriate for peacekeeping duty. This assumption goes beyond those constraints, imposed by international political considerations, that make major powers unsuitable peacekeeping participants. Rather, there is the additional presumption that the military personnel themselves of major powers—compared to those of neutral middle powers—are less adaptable to the restricted and impartial use of force inherent in the peacekeeping mission and are less likely to give allegiance to an international body.

To what degree the presumed peacekeeping inefficacy of major-power soldiers is factually the case is an issue of both theoretical and practical import. It has been shown that behavioral compliance to impartial and noncoercive practices in on-duty performance was uniform throughout all UNFICYP units, British and non-British alike. It was also argued that the constabulary ethic was primarily engendered by the common field situation rather than by any peculiar national proclivities toward minimal use of force. The question remains, nevertheless, of whether the British soldiers, at least subjectively or in private, were less committed to peacekeeping than their fellow soldiers from the neutral middle powers. By separating out the British responses to the peacekeeping items covered in the interviews, some evidence can be offered on this question.

Given in table 9 are contrasts between British UNFICYP and other UNFICYP military officers along with the three peacekeeping variables of constabulary ethic, internationalism, and peacekeeping evaluations. The British are somewhat less likely (44 percent) to give constabulary responses than other UNFICYP

Table 9. Comparison of British and Other UNFICYP Officers by Selected Peacekeeping Variables (Percentages)

	British UNFICYP Officers (N = 25)	Other UNFICYP Officers (N = 85)
Report constabulary ethic	44	53
Give internationalist responses	52	65
Evaluate UNFICYP as a success	76	73

officers (53 percent). Also, on the question of attitude change toward international bodies following UNFICYP assignment, the British officers were similarly somewhat less likely than non-British officers to give internationalist responses: 52 percent compared to 65 percent. On the evaluations of the success of the United Nations operation in Cyprus, British versus non-British differences were insignificant.

It is a matter of interpretation as to what conclusion is to be drawn from these data bearing upon the proposition that soldiers coming from major powers—with military organizations shaped by warfare—are less predisposed toward peacekeeping tasks than those from neutral middle powers. There was a tendency, though only a slight one, for the British UNFICYP officers to be somewhat more constrained in articulating peacekeeping sentiments. But this slight tendency for a more conventional characterization of the soldierly role among the British officers was not of the magnitude to warrant the assertion that soldiers coming from armies where the warrior role has been predominant are less capable of or adaptable to peacekeeping tasks than those of smaller countries where peacekeeping is more the military norm. Certainly, at the all important level of constabulary practices, and perhaps even at the subjective level of peacekeeping commitment, conventionally trained soldiers from major powers—at least as demonstrated by the British participation in UNFICYP—can well be regarded as possessing the potential for exemplary peace soldiers.

Dynamics of
Peacekeeping
Attitudes

8

Academic definitions as well as ideological attitudes as to the military's propriety and efficacy in international peacekeeping missions fluctuate between two poles. At one pole are those for whom the armed forces are incorrigibly unfit for constabulary roles as well as rigidly locked into parochial allegiances. At the other are those who see military personnel as quite accommodative to constabulary precepts and correspondingly adaptable to international loyalties. In a real sense, these two viewpoints differ about whether armed forces are to be understood as a profession whose very raison d'être is the application of coercive violence for partial cause, or whether military personnel are the most feasible practitioners of the still to be charted requirements of impartial peacekeeping. Neither conception is wholly wrong or wholly accurate. Rather, the issue should be reformulated as to how novel peacekeeping standards impact upon notions of continuing military institutional identity. Although the presentation up to this point has implicitly been sensitive to these issues, we now address ourselves to a more directly analytical examination of the dynamics of peacekeeping attitudes among serving United Nations military officers.

Attitude Formation Over Time

Along with the findings based on participant observation and the 110 interviews of UNFICYP officers presented in previous chapters, panel interview data—repeated interviews with the same respondent—were collected from 25 UNFICYP officers. Such panel interviews are especially suitable for ascertaining changes in viewpoints over time—in this study, presumably, changes that are a reflection of the effects of United Nations service on attitude formation toward peacekeeping. All of the panel interviews were with officers assigned to national contingents with six-month determinate tours. Each respondent was interviewed three times; at the beginnning, middle, and end of his UNFICYP assignment. Specifically, the panel interviews were conducted within the first month of the officer's arrival on Cyprus, the third or fourth month of the tour, and during the final month of UNFICYP duty (most often the final two weeks).

The findings of the panel interviews are summarized in table 10 with regard to the three key peacekeeping attitudinal variables—constabulary ethic, internationalism, and evaluation of UNFICYP. In sum, the panel interview findings corroborate the field observations discussed earlier: the discreteness and independent nature of the peacekeeping variables. Indeed, the picture that emerges is one of discontinuity, if not contradiction, in the relation and formation of the key peace-keeping attitudes.

We can see from table 10 that the constabulary ethic increased linearly over the course of the UNFICYP tour: 32 percent reported it during the first month, 40 percent during the middle two months, and 60 percent during the final month. Among the panel interviewees, that is, the constabulary ethic almost doubled

Table 10. Attitude Changes of UNFICYP Officers by Selected Peacekeeping Variables (25 Panel Interviews, Percentages)

| | Length of UNFICYP Tour | | |
	First Month	Three-to-four Months	Sixth Month
Report constabulary ethic	32	40	60
Give internationalist responses	56	36	24
Evaluate UNFICYP as a success	88	44	72

over the period of their Cyprus assignments. It will be remembered that the constabulary ethic was operationalized to refer to all respondents who believed that more than traditional military skills were required for peacekeeping duty and that peacekeeping effectiveness did not require the use of force. It is to be stressed again, however, that the privately held opinions of UNFICYP officers—whether for or against abstract constabulary principles—coexisted with near universal behavioral adherence to constabulary standards in the field. But the panel interview data do show that over the course of the UNFICYP tour there was an increasing correspondence between attitudinal and behavioral measures on the constabulary ethic.

The measure of attitudes toward internationalism was based on the UNFICYP officer's favorable or unfavorable regard of the United Nations in particular and international bodies in general. In table 10, internationalist responses include those from officers whose attitudes did not change vis-à-vis internationalist bodies as well as responses from officers who stated they had become more favorable. We find that 56 percent of the officers gave internationalist responses during the first phase of their tours, 36 percent at the time of the second interview, and only 24 percent by the end of their UNFICYP tours. Put in another way, about three-quarters of the panel interviewees had developed negative attitudes toward international bodies, as exemplified by the United Nations, by the time they returned to their home countries. This decline in internationalism over the course of an UNFICYP tour was one of the most striking attitudinal changes among United Nations military officers at the line contingent level.[1]

The third peacekeeping variable was based on the officer's evaluation of UNFICYP as a concrete peacekeeping enterprise. Given in table 10 are the percentages of the panel interviewees who termed UNFICYP as either a partial or complete success. In the initial interviews, 88 percent judged UNFICYP to be a success. This dropped sharply to 44 percent during the middle period. But by the time of the final interview, 72 percent again stated they regarded the United Nations in Cyprus as essentially successful. Thus, unlike the linear patterns of attitude formation for the other two peacekeeping variables—increasing constabulary ethic, decreasing internationalism—evaluations of UNFICYP reflected a cyclical variation: from high to low and back to high.

For an assessment of the interrelationships between the three peacekeeping variables the interview data must be understood in the context of the field observations. We find, first, that attitude formations with regard to the constabulary ethic and internationalism are inversely correlated. Thus, while universal constabulary behavior persists and constabulary attitudes increase, internationalism quite consistently declines. The formation of these peacekeeping attitudinal variables, moreover, involves different processes. The increasing proportion of officers giving constabulary responses over the course of their UNFICYP tours is further evidence in support of the proposition that field experiences, rather than pre-UNFICYP socialization or personal background traits, account for the emergence of the constabulary ethic. That is, it appears that the very act of performing in a constabulary manner serves to shape attitudes in the same direction. Moreover, the constabulary ethic was also consistent with the stated policies of UNFICYP as enunciated in United Nations enabling resolutions and local UNFICYP standard operating procedures.

The decline in internationalism, on the other hand, occurs despite official espousal of United Nations priorities in, of course, UNFICYP itself and even to some degree at the formal level of the contributing nation. The exceptions to this generalization—the UNFICYP officers whose internationalism increased—will be treated separately below. But it is relevant at this point to remember that there was a generic strain between military officers and UNFICYP civilian officials, and this was undoubtedly the chief factor contributing to the decline of internationalism among UNFICYP officers. Yet it should also be remembered from the interview data based on the entire sample that the internationalist sentiments of the contingent line officers were markedly lower than those of the headquarters staff. Thus we seem to have a situation in which officers not in direct working association with the United Nations civilian staff were also the most likely to report increasingly negative attitudes toward the United Nations. Indirect confrontation rather than familiarity seems to have been the breeding ground for much of the contempt for international bodies and their officialdom displayed by UNFICYP military officers. Or, put in another way, where the increase in the constabulary ethic derived primarily from the immediate field situation, the decline in internationalism also displayed by UNFICYP officers was generated by conflict sources one step removed from the nexus of civil-military contacts within UNFICYP.

The turnabouts on evaluation of UNFICYP over the course of a six-month tour also require some explication. The initially high evaluation of UNFICYP largely reflected a form of naive idealism as to the prerogatives and effectiveness of a United Nations operation in resolving the Cyprus dispute. Once the officers confronted the limits of UNFICYP as a military force and the obduracy of the Cypriots, however, a period of marked disillusionment set in. (For many lower-grade officers and other ranks the phase of disillusionment persisted through the end of their tours and beyond.) Typically, however, by the end of the tour, a favorable evaluation of UNFICYP reemerged but this time grounded in a more realistic awareness of the United Nations contribution to peace within the operational limits of the UNFICYP mission. Where the initial period was based on the desire for a permanent solution adjudicated if not enforced by the United Nations, the final period was a recognition of the practical import of the sheer maintenance of the peace without necessarily bringing about a permanent resolution of either the Cypriot inter-communal conflict or the potential war between Greece and Turkey. In point of theory, such a pragmatic understanding of the peacekeeping role can be construed as another element of the constabulary ethic.

We note also that it was in the initial phase of the UNFICYP tour that the panel respondents gave high marks to UNFICYP peacekeeping success as well as reported their highest levels of internationalism; yet in the final phase, high evaluations of UNFICYP accompanied low levels of internationalism. This immediately suggests, as was borne out in the field observations and interview responses, that the attitudinal relationships between internationalism and UNFICYP evaluations entailed contrasting dynamics over the course of the Cyprus tour. Thus, it was found that evaluation of UNFICYP success during the initial period tended to adopt the United Nations sui generis as the prime reference and to encompass the entire Cyprus situation. But by the end of their tours, when internationalism was lowest, the officers defined UNFICYP success almost exclusively in terms of the efficacy of their own national contingents in their respective zones of responsibility. Or, put in another way, the referent shifted from strategic to tactical standards of peacekeeping success. Finally, in this regard, it must be mentioned that there was little increase in national chauvinism among UNFICYP officers over the course of the Cyprus tour. What seemed to be occurring was the development of a kind of "all in the same boat" mentality which simultaneously corresponded with heightened hostility toward the United Nations. Perhaps it would be more accurate to term the attitude formation of UNFICYP officers as becoming less supranational while becoming more transnational.

Becoming an Internationalist: The UNFICYP Exceptions

Although the overwhelming majority of military officers did not report an increase in their internationalist sentiments following UNFICYP assignment, we direct our attention now to the exceptions to the general pattern: the UNFICYP officers who did become more internationalist. The logical and methodological structure adopted in the analysis here is based on a developmental structure. This mode of analysis has been variously termed, "the quest for universals," "the genetic perspective," or, most commonly "analytic induction."[2] Unlike in the conventional handling of statistical data, the analytic induction method seeks to provide causal understanding by providing a sequential model of progressively accumulating factors which in their total combination account for the emergence of the phenomena under consideration. Although the analytic induction method has been customarily used to explain types of social deviancy (drug addiction, marijuana smoking, embezzlement, membership in apocalyptic cults), this procedure lends itself to a causal explanation of the emergence of internationalism among certain UNFICYP officers.

Indeed, in a manner of speaking, the UNFICYP military officers who became internationalists were "deviants" in that they contrasted sharply with the prevailing norms of the UNFICYP officer corps.

The explanation of the emergence of an internationalist perspective among a minority of UNFICYP officers incorporates a causal sequence of factors which pertain to predisposing conditions (attributes of the officer prior to his contact with UNFICYP) and situational contingencies (conditions of social interaction within UNFICYP). The sequential arrangement of the factors may be conceived as a funnel which systematically reduces the number of officers who can be considered available to become internationalists and at the same time increasingly specifies who is available. In theory at least, all officers assigned to UNFICYP could be considered as potential internationalists. But each factor serves both to narrow the range of officers available and to show why only a small number ultimately became internationalists. Four such factors will be presented for the development of an internationalist identity among UNFICYP officers.

All told, twenty-five of the UNFICYP officers from among the total 110 samples reported they had become more internationalist since assignment to UNFICYP. Yet in further questioning only fourteen of these stated they would actually give higher priority to the demands of the United Nations over those of their home countries—in the hypothetical situation that there would be such a conflict. This core group of UNFICYP internationalists thereby became the subject of the analytic induction method. It was not possible to obtain complete data pertinent to all four steps on the emergence of internationalism for all fourteen UNFICYP officers who were classified as internationalists. However, full information on all four factors was available for ten officers. All known data for the other internationalist officers conformed to the sequential model, and inferences about unknown items, based on what information did exist, indicated that these too met each condition. For the conceptual presentation of the sequential model it would be desirable to present individual biographical information for at least some of the internationalist officers. But in order to maintain the anonymity of the respondents, the exposition that follows relies on general and occasionally vague description. As a prefatory remark, however, it can be noted that all of the major contributing nations to UNFICYP were represented among the UNFICYP internationalists, and these internationalists tended to be concentrated among the older UNFICYP officers.

An initial predisposing condition shared by all of the eventual UNFICYP internationalists was that their career advancement in their home armies was essentially limited even before the possibilities of assignment to UNFICYP appeared. There was a candid and realistic awareness that chances for further promotion were minimal. Thus when the opportunity for United Nations service arose, such duty was seen at worst as a lateral grade transfer or at best as an opportunity to obtain favorable recognition in a new setting. In cold fact, some UNFICYP internationalists would have been on the retirement list had they remained in their home armies. Complimenting the personal willingness of these military officers to accept a peacekeeping assignment, there was also the structural factor that home military establishments tended to select for extended United Nations duty those very officers whose careers were no longer in the mainstream.[3]

A second predisposing condition of the eventual internationalists was that their personal situations had reached a point where the option of any relocation abroad became an attraction. Factors such as the ill fortunes of marriage, or the maturity of one's children, or the growing punishment of northern winters on middle-aged bones were all conducive to a kind of "itchiness" prior to the UNFICYP opportunity. Moreover, it was apparent that United Nations peacekeeping was easily interpreted as more prestigious than humdrum duty in small armies, themselves undergoing an erosion of legitimacy in their home societies. There was also the elemental fact that UN duty would be financially more remunerative than remaining at home, what with UN allowances, tax benefits, and the lower cost of living in Cyprus. But it should be stressed that prior to UNFICYP duty these predisposing conditions—whether a "push" from one's personal life or the "pull" of the cachet of United Nations service—contributed only to a nascent rather than to a fully realized internationalism.

Sequentially following the two predisposing conditions, the third step toward the development of an internationalist identity revolved around situational contingencies within UNFICYP itself. The officers who became internationalists were all in positions which initially or subsequently could be converted into extended UNFICYP assignments. Typically this involved a headquarters staff position, though in a few cases a line officer could arrange repeated six-month tours. Of course, such extended UNFICYP tours would only confirm the officer's removal from the main career paths of his home army. Under these conditions, peacekeeping was increasingly seen as a surrogate career. Acquiring a good performance record in UNFICYP was regarded not as a requisite for advancement back home but as an entry credential into the pool of international military officers from which truce observers and allied specialists were drawn to staff the multitude of smaller United Nations peacekeeping missions. Thus internationalism dovetailed with changing career plans. Moreover, unlike in the line contingents, where the United Nations was often held in dubious regard, in the headquarters staff the officer with propensities toward internationalism would find such views mutually reinforced by most of his fellow staff members.

Yet one final step was required in the progression of factors making for an internationalist. UNFICYP duty had to be regarded as rewarding in its own right. Most important in this regard were the psychic rewards derived from being privy to and part of the management of crises—big and small. For those assigned to the headquarters staff, there could be a sense of immediate and ongoing accomplishment typically unavailable to the line officer at the contingent level. There was, moreover, the appeal of frequently meeting and observing visiting United Nations dignitaries, high-level diplomats, mass-media reporters, and the leaders of the Cypriot communities. And one must make mention of the obvious benefits of the usually short workday at headquarters and the concomitant freedom to pursue one's leisure interests. Even from a detached viewpoint, how many positions could one realistically hope to attain which could compare favorably with peacekeeping at UNFICYP headquarters in terms of remuneration, work conditions, and intrinsic job satisfaction? The capstone of becoming an internationalist, then, was in the UNFICYP officer's acknowledgment of the occupational rewards of the peacekeeping assignment.

To sum up, the natural history of the UNFICYP officer who became an internationalist followed an invariable progression through four sequential conditions: (1) career stagnation in the home national army; (2) personal predisposition to relocate abroad; (3) placement in a position allowing for extended UNFICYP duty (typically at the headquarters staff); and (4) a positive experience in the peacekeeping assignment. All of the internationalists went through each stage in order, and none of those who retained primary loyalty to their home nation went through the same progression of conditions. The four-stage model presented, therefore, seems to be both necessary and sufficient cause of internationalism. We repeat that the definition of an internationalist included those who stated that their internationalist perspectives increased over the course of the UNFICYP tour to the extent that they were willing to give more allegiance to the United Nations than to their home country.

The emergence of an internationalist identity meeting these stringent criteria was generated by a serial conjunction of evolving pragmatic responses to changing situational contingencies; responses which over time resulted in a redefinition of the appropriate social context in which individual advantage would be maximal—from a national to an international structure. What is noteworthy in the etiology of internationalism within a segment of the UNFICYP officer corps is that the ascendancy of internationalist over nationalist allegiance did not intrinsically involve moral or ideological considerations.[4] This is not in any way an aspersion on the quality or integrity of the UNFICYP internationalists. For whatever the causes underlying their conversion to internationalism, such UNFICYP officers were to become the mainstay of a smoothly operating peacekeeping force. Nor is this to be construed, even, as a belittlement of the motives of the UNFICYP internationalists. For, certainly, motivations derived from personal convenience and individual interests equally described the large majority of UNFICYP officers who remained nationalists. But it is to say that noble ideals were no more characteristic of the internationalists than they were of the nationalists. To put it in a more positive way, high levels of peacekeeping performance characterized nearly all UNFICYP officers regardless of their political loyalties.

Soldierly Honor and the Constabulary Ethic

The dynamics in peacekeeping attitude formation were nowhere more evident than in the reconciliation of notions of soldierly honor with the constabulary ethic. For despite the behavioral adherence of UNFICYP soldiers to constabulary standards in the field, there was a fundamental tension between the values of the traditional warrior role and the peacekeeping precepts of absolute minimal force. Some cognitive dissonance could be reduced by redefining peacekeeping duty to conform to the conventional soldierly model. In the words of a British officer:

Peacekeeping in its very nature is what the British soldier has been doing all over the world. UN duty is not all that different from what had to be done in Aden, Malaya, Hong Kong, and you name it. The men are doing what they've always done—and they do it damn well because they're real soldiers. Whether you call it peacekeeping or soldiering depends on the eye of the beholder.

Conversely, the military could be redefined to match the requirements of peacekeeping. As one Canadian officer put it:

Peacekeeping makes the army over into a positive rather than a negative force in history. An army that is always at war might have combat experience. But is that good for peacekeeping? You need an army of trained men who are not used to shooting at everything. Killing is not the sign of a good army. Peacekeeping brings out the qualities of the best soldier. We just have to change our outmoded ideas as to what makes a soldier.

The self-definitional disjuncture between the soldier and the peacekeeper was, or course, most applicable to those members of the United Nations force who were regular soldiers; but to some degree these antinomies were embodied throughout UNFICYP. How these normative contradictions were handled by UNFICYP soldiers is reflected in the diversity of viewpoints found in the representative comments given below.

A British noncommissioned officer: "One thing makes a soldier different and better than anybody else. The thing which gives that dignity which nobody else can have is his respect for the man he is fighting. No civilian can ever have that. No soldier who hasn't fought can have it either. In peacekeeping the trouble is that you don't have any enemy, and this means you don't have any dignity as a soldier."

A British officer: "I know quite a few senior officers who are ashamed to wear a UN ribbon. For someone who has been through World War II and practically everywhere else, a UN ribbon looks kind of silly. It demeans real battle ribbons. But the promise of a UN ribbon is what I use to keep the privates in line here."

A Canadian officer: "The toughest job is how to shift a soldier from all the aggression we've been teaching him to telling him he can't be a fighter anymore. Even in peacekeeping you need some trouble to keep the men happy. The more trouble there is, the more everybody enjoys peacekeeping. Without trouble peacekeeping runs against the grain of the soldier."

An Irish soldier: "I like being in the field. I like getting dirty and hearing men curse. I like to watch the lads with last night's KEO [a local Cyprus beer] in their guts running over the hills. You can get this in peacekeeping just as in war. What matters is you feel like a man. Then when I go back home I can enjoy the old lady and family."

A Finnish officer: "The problem is always to be on top of the soldier who is trained—let's face it—to kill. UNFICYP is a paradox. The army is for war and the UN is for peace. That is a contradiction. It is a good thing the Finnish character is suitable for peacekeeping. We can take many insults. It takes a lot to arouse us. Nothing gets us excited. You take that farm boy there. He doesn't know too much about what's going on, but he won't

get excited. Ninety percent of this job is not getting excited.
That's why we Finns are psychologically suited for keeping the
peace. Only soldiers with this temperament can be
peacekeepers.''

The salience of conventional notions of soldierly honor in the
self-conceptions of UNFICYP military personnel was revealed as
well from a different vantage. For despite the common peacekeeping mission, a topic of frequent conversation involved invi-
dious comparisions of the military prowess and organizational
qualities of the various national contingents.

A Danish officer: ''Our men are not collected from the slums
of their countries. They are volunteers who have been carefully
picked. They are the cream of the crop and a much higher grade
of men than you would find in a regular group of soldiers. The
British have an army to solve their unemployment problems. The
Black Watch aren't soldiers, they're lumberjacks and timbermen
from Canada. These are men who can't make a living at home and
bring their troubles into the army. Just compare our soldiers'
intelligence and manners with the Brits and the Irish and the
Canadians.''

A Canadian officer: ''The Canadians and British are the only real
soldiers here. The Irish are a sloppy army. The Danes and Finns
are really civilians in uniform here for a vacation in the sun. The
Swedes with their beards and necklaces are a hippy army.''

A British officer: ''How can you seriously compare a unit like
the Pompadours with the others except the Black Watch. We and
the Canadians are an army. The others are a mixed batch of
civilian tourists, half-soldiers, and a few professionals who never
fought a war.''

A Swedish officer: ''What do they mean we have had no war in
150 years? Over three thousand soldiers fought with the Finns
during the Winter War. Wasn't the Congo combat? And if there
are no wars to fight, the officer can still be a hero by leading his
men to climb mountains. If you listen to the British talk, you
think every British officer was at Dunkirk. How many of them do
you think really have been in a war?''

Yet, when all is said and done, the martial stereotypes of the various national contingents were beside the cardinal point of peacekeeping efficacy. To be sure, speculation abounded as to what contingent contrasts might appear if the UNFICYP troops were required to carry out coercive enforcement actions. But despite the topical concern with relative military prowess, the comparative combat effectiveness of the contingents was basically irrelevant. In any all-out war, the United Nations forces would almost surely be overwhelmed by the superior forces of Greek or Turkish Cypriots, and certainly would be if the armed forces of the Cypriots' mainland patrons entered the fray. From the standpoint of peacekeeping capabilities, the issue really rests on how the criteria of impartiality and minimal force were met. The striking thing about UNFICYP—regardless of differences in military background, national character, or prior peacekeeping orientation—was the uniformly successful peacekeeping performance of all the national contingents. On this score, certainly, contemporary standards of military professonalism were quite compatible with the constabulary ethic.

The Sociology of
Peace Soldiers

The interpretations of the UNFICYP findings have been pur-
posively framed to have broader applicability to peacekeeping
forces in general. In contrast with the conventional historical or
case study approaches, the sociological endeavor seeks to formu-
late propositions necessarily several steps removed from particular-
ized description. Although such a disciplinary bias can lead to the
loss of concrete detail, it is, one hopes, at the gain of more
analytical understanding. The point is that ultimately a sociological analysis of peacekeeping forces must address the internal
dynamics and broader conditions which contribute to the reconstruction of an institution—armed forces—heretofore instruments
of partiality and coercive violence. To the degree that sociological
findings are incorporated into this reconstruction, the social
researcher becomes part of the process of institution building.
Such a role becomes obligatory in the present period when
peacekeeping operations appear to be in the ascendancy. Moreover, the very military establishments which are most liable for
peacekeeping duties are often the same ones which are undergoing institutional redefinition in the wake of eroding traditional
supports of military legitimacy.

We return then to the constabulary model of the military from
which the concept of the peace soldier directly derives. In contrast
with standard armed forces, the constabulary and peace soldier are
concerned with the attainment of viable political compromises
rather than with the resolution of conflict through force. Where

standard armed forces are typically dedicated to efficient achievement of military victory without regard to nonmilitary considerations, the constabulary and peace soldier are charged with maintaining the peace even to the detriment of military considerations.
But while the constabulary model encompasses the peace soldier,
it does not define the peace soldier. In the manner that the
constabulary model is an accentuation of emergent norms in
military professionalism, the peace soldier is a further accentuation of the constabulary model. Where the constabulary model
conforms to the notion of military service in accordance with
national goals, the peace soldier is committed to impartiality
under the mandate of an international body. Where the constabulary model allows for measured if minimal force to
achieve political ends, the peace soldier resorts to force only in
self-defense.

Because the concept of the peace soldier permits the use of force
only in the cause of self-defense, an explication of what is meant
by self-defense is required. And precisely because there can be no
hard-and-fast definition of self-defense in the field context of
peacekeeping, the concept of the peace soldier suffers certain
ambiguities. But over the two decades in which United Nations
military forces have been deployed, some ground rules can be
discerned on the operational meaning of self-defense in peacekeeping assignments. There is an implied distinction between
self-defense of the *person* and self-defense of the *mission*. Self-
defense of the person is always allowable. Indeed, it would be very
doubtful if any nation would contribute its soldiers to a peacekeeping force without this minimal guarantee of recourse to
arms.

Self-defense of mission, however, is much more problematical.
What seems to be peacekeeping doctrine on this issue is that,
while fire cannot be initiated under any circumstances by UN
troops, such troops can be ordered to perform missions which may
draw fire. In that event, return fire may be allowable. But pursuit
of mission can, and typically will, give way to withdrawal if the
likelihood of sustaining attack is too great. If the mission is to be
pursued, however, the peacekeeping commander must seek to

maneuver his men initially into a tactically defensive posture from which armed self-defense then becomes permissible. To complicate matters, such maneuvering must be perceived to be in accord with the canons of impartiality. Calculations become very fine indeed when trying to determine what are the outer boundaries to which a peacekeeping mission can be pushed without invoking attack. That peace soldiers have generally not pushed beyond these boundaries reflects both their professionalism and the realities of the superior military force with which they are usually confronted.

The limitations of the peace soldier as a paragon for military forces must be realistically acknowledged. While the constabulary model in the form of national armies is in accord with ascendant norms of military professionalism, the peace soldier serving under international command will play only a subsidiary role in the total structure of contemporary armed forces. Moreover, where the constabulary model in national armies allows for the retention of some degree of independence from the environment, the peace soldier is ultimately—and some would say fatally—bound by the acceptance of his role on the part of involved disputants. If this acceptance is withdrawn before political solutions are realized, the peace soldier, akin to the emperor with no clothes, stands naked before whirling power plays. But this reflects more on the maleficence of the world order than it does on the professional qualities of the peace soldier. Even under the constraints which restrict a peacekeeping force, the peace soldier still merits our close attention. He merits this attention not only for the concrete uses to which he is put in United Nations service but also as an ideal standard for emergent military professionalism at large, an ideal which in the UNFICYP case was closely realized. For in contrast with the conventional soldier, the peace soldier—the extreme ramification of the constabulary ethic—favors persuasion over punishment, compromise over capitulation, and perseverance over conquest.

The findings offered in this study have steered a course between the stereotyping of military personnel as incapable of adaptation to the novel requirements of the peacekeeping task and the idealizing of peacekeeping personnel as internationally motivated constabularies. Peace soldiers are neither hidebound warriors nor one-world altruists. Rather, the UNFICYP soldiers represented collectively—with little variation between nationalities—military personnel who increasingly accepted minimal force precepts, who withheld final allegiance to the United Nations, and whose evaluations of peacekeeping evolved from naive optimism through cynical disillusionment to an eventual realistically favorable appreciation. Precisely because these findings run counter to many of the characterizations of peacekeeping soldiers in the extant literature, it becomes appropriate to reconsider the propositions summarized in the introductory chapter. In light of the UNFICYP empirical evidence, that is, the propositional inventory of the sociology of peace soldiers can now be reformulated in the following manner.

1. *Behavioral adherence to constabulary peacekeeping standards is not exclusively characteristic of soldiers coming from middle neutral powers.* One of the most striking features of the UNFICYP force was the absence of any observable behavioral differences across all national contingents in meeting constabulary standards. In no case was any one nationality more or less likely to depart from rigid adherence to impartiality and absolute minimum use of force. Especially noteworthy, UNFICYP was an exceptional peacekeeping force in that it did include a major power component—Britcon. Yet, the peacekeeping behavior of the British officers and men was indistinguishable from that of soldiers coming from neutral middle powers—the Nordic countries, Canada, and Ireland. Even on the attitudinal level, the British peacekeepers were only slightly less likely to give constabulary responses than were their counterparts from neutral middle powers. This all indicates that the adaptation of armed forces to meet the criteria of constabulary norms is largely independent of preconditional factors such as traditions of international involvement and aggressive warfare. There is little support for the contention that the political-military milieu of contributing nations has any direct bearing on the propensity of its soldiers to use force in the peacekeeping assignment.

This is not to gainsay the realities of international politics which do make neutral middle powers the appropriate and primary reserve for peacekeeping forces. Nor is it to say that all national armies in all cases are equally adept at performing peacekeeping missions. But it does not follow that the military establishments of neutral middle powers have any social organizational advantages for peacekeeping compared with those of major powers. Nor do soldiers from major powers, at least as typified by the British soldiers in UNFICYP, necessarily compare unfavorably in their constabulary suitability with soldiers from military establishments which have not been recently involved in armed interventions and wars.

2. *Adaptation and adherence to constabulary standards derives from commonly shared peacekeeping experiences in the field following assignment to a United Nations force, rather than from prior peacekeeping training and orientation.* The uniformly successful adaptation to constabulary standards displayed throughout UNFICYP was all the more remarkable in light of the differences in the recruitment policies and military formats between the national contingents. But, what is very important, the uniform constabulary behavior also occurred in the context of considerable variation in the amount of specialized peacekeeping training received by the contingents prior to their arrival in Cyprus, ranging from intensive (Cancon, Swedcon, Dancon) through nominal (Fincon, Ircon) to virtually none (Britcon). What the UNFICYP contingents did share in common, however, was the actual peacekeeping experience itself. And, as the participant observation revealed, the constabulary ethic was an outcome of on-duty, in-the-field experiences.[1] This central finding was corroborated by panel interview data which demonstrated the increasing salience of constabulary precepts over the course of the UNFICYP tour.

Indeed, the possibility suggests itself that certain kinds of prior peacekeeping orientation may retard the emergence of a constabulary ethic once the soldier is placed in an actual peacekeeping situation. This would be to the degree that peacekeeping designees acquire false expectations of their local acceptance or are led to believe the peacekeeping force will be fully efficacious in realizing permanent solutions. But whatever the possibility of such unintended negative effects, the UNFICYP soldiers became effective constabularies independent of—or perhaps in spite of—prior peacekeeping training.² The determining factor in the forging of the constabulary ethic was in the informal learning arising out of the field situation, coupled with stringent United Nations minimum-of-force policies.

3. *Participation in a United Nations force does not foster internationalist values on the part of peacekeeping soldiers.* Contrary to much of the accepted wisdom in the peacekeeping literature, peace soldiers do not appear to become more internationalist over the length of their United Nations service. Somewhat over a third of the UNFICYP officers reported they became less internationalist following their initial arrival on Cyprus, while slightly under a quarter stated they had become more internationalist; the remainder indicated their views toward international authority had not changed. More directly, the panel interview data clearly revealed a decreasing internationalist identity over the course of the UNFICYP tour. True, as was discussed in special detail, some of the officers became bona fide internationalists, but these were the exceptions to United Nations military service, not its products. Moreover, although based on less firm evidence, the internationalism of the UNFICYP other ranks, if anything, declined even more markedly than that documented for the officer corps.

With regard to the proposition that soldiers from neutral middle powers are more disposed to subscribe to internationalist values than their major power counterparts, the evidence is not definitive. Although British UNFICYP officers were slightly less likely to report internationalist sentiments than officers from the other nationalities, intraorganizational differences, regardless of nationality, accounted for much of the internationalist variance. Thus headquarters staff officers were three times more likely to identify favorably with the United Nations than were the line contingent officers. It is to be remembered that the general decline in internationalism within the UNFICYP officer corps was more in the nature of increasing skepticism toward international bodies (that is, the United Nations) than in any increase in hostility toward other UNFICYP contributing nations. The UNFICYP findings, that is, are witness to a decline in supranationalism with no accompanying decrease in transnationalism.[3] But again, as with the constabulary ethic, it was the commonality of the UNFICYP experience rather than preexisting nationality differences that had the strongest effect on the formation of peacekeeping attitudes.

4. *Internationalist values and the constabulary ethic do not constitute or derive from a common attitudinal factor.* A persistent assumption in the peacekeeping literature is the treatment of the commitment to noncoercive measures and allegiance to supranational bodies as twin facets of an overarching and indivisible peacekeeping factor. The research of this study most clearly refutes this assumption. The UNFICYP findings not only revealed the constabulary ethic and internationalism to be quite discrete variables but also as covarying in opposition to each other. Rather than operating in the tandem manner of a positive manifold, increasing commitment to constabulary practices paralleled decreasing international values. The relationship between these two variables is, of course, one of inverse correlation and not cause and effect. Thus it would be misleading in the extreme to say that internationalism impedes constabulary behavior. What can be said is that soldierly performance in an impartial and noncoercive fashion is not predicated on one-world or related internationalist beliefs. Stated in more formal terms, internationalism is neither a necessary nor sufficient condition of constabulary peacekeeping behavior.

5. *Contemporary standards of military professionalism are readily adaptable to the requirements of the peacekeeping role.* The leitmotiv of the peacekeeping literature is the ultimate disjuncture between military professionalism and peacekeeping requirements. Yet what was striking in the UNFICYP officer corps was how that very military professionalism contributed to, rather than handicapped, an adaptation to the constabulary model. To be sure, the dominant social and political conservatism of the modern military professional—as was also evidenced in the UNFICYP officer corps—might seemingly work against the norms of the peacekeeping role; but the empirical data show this convincingly not to have been the case. Also true, there was some private expression of resentment over the limitations imposed on

the use of force, but the overriding reality was how capably the United Nations soldiers performed their peacekeeping assignments in an impartial and noncoercive manner. It is a gross misunderstanding to consider the glory of war as an essential ingredient of military honor.[4] It is similarly erroneous to consider the requirements of peacekeeping as in contradiction with military professionalism. Rather than giving weight to preconceptions of an inflexible "military mind," what is needed is a more grounded understanding of the norms of military professionalism.[5] For if anything, the UNFICYP evidence shows how adaptable the officers were to peacekeeping practices within an underlying context of military professionalism.

It becomes appropriate, then, to conclude with a statement on how military professionalism can conform with the requirements of the peace soldier. Even more than standard armed forces, peacekeeping forces are not to be conceived as a static model but as a dynamic process which engenders social organizational restructuring in response to changing conditions. Following the conceptual leads of Morris Janowitz, modern military professionalism is increasingly responsive to an ascendant managerial expertise with concomitant lessened salience—though not disappearance—of elements of heroic leadership.[6] This corresponds with an organizational trend within modern armed forces from a form of authority based on traditional styles of domination to newer forms of managerial philosophy stressing persuasive incentives, personal manipulation, and consensus. In these terms, peacekeeping is clearly a progression of military professionalism along managerial lines. Being the pragmatic military professional he is, the peace soldier is shaped by the concrete needs and demands of an immediate peacekeeping situation within the limits suited to and tolerated by the international mandate under which he serves. The peace soldier is one who is able to subscribe to the precepts of absolute minimal force, a reliance on compromise and negotiation, and the recognition of the elusiveness of permanent political solutions.

Although, in the peacekeeping context, the brilliant strategist or forceful tactician becomes obsolete, elements of heroic leadership do reappear, albeit in nonaggressive guise. Most important, despite the pacific connotations associated with the routine peacekeeping tasks of impartial monitoring and interpositioning between opposing disputants, such duties in real life can often call for demonstrations of sheer physical courage. Moreover, despite the feature of modern military professionalism which entails mastery over increasingly complex technical systems, contemporary peacekeeping forces represent the anomalous case of managing weaponry basically unchanged from that of a generation ago. And it is probably the case that the handling of readily comprehensible weaponry allows for another consistency between heroic self-images and the peacekeeping role. Furthermore, the primitive living conditions of soldiering in the field, the requirements of troop leadership in operational situations, and the ultimate recourse to arms in the always possible event of withstanding assault, are all peacekeeping variants of the heroic model. Thus, while the concept of the constabulary force reflects in the main the emergent managerial norms of military professionalism, it also accommodates itself to more traditional aspects of soldierly honor.

But the most dominant traditional characteristic of the military professionalism of the UN peace soldiers was their maintenance of primary allegiance to their home nationality. It would be very premature to regard military professionalism in peacekeeping forces as a modern form of the nonnational armies of premodern Europe. For in addition to the nationalist attitudes uncovered in the interview data, there was also the noticeable propensity among the line contingents of UNFICYP to reaffirm national military traditions through repeated and extended forms of parades, ceremonies, and ritualism. Even peacekeeping service itself, moreover, was typically interpreted as serving national military purpose: the opportunity for operational deployment in an overseas environment, the acquisition of experience in multinational military cooperation, and a rationale for an armed forces establishment to counter antimilitary domestic opinion. Yet this root nationalism of the United Nations military officers was not incompatible with peacekeeping professionalism.

The peace soldiers of the United Nations are not without paradoxes. Trained in the skills of fighting and lethal weaponry, they proved to be readily adaptable to the practices of the constabulary ethic. Maintaining final loyalty to their home nations, they performed in an impartial manner under the authority of an international world body. Simultaneously required to chart and conform to the imperatives of a novel military role, they reconciled soldierly honor with the peacekeeping task. Yet because of, rather than in spite of, these seeming contradictions, the institution building of viable peacekeeping forces has been facilitated by the standards of modern military professionalism.

The paradoxical qualities of the emergent constabulary role are succinctly captured in what has become the unofficial motto of the United Nations soldier: ''Peacekeeping is not a soldier's job, but only a soldier can do it.''

Postscript

Events in Cyprus took a dramatic and distressing turn just as this manuscript was in the final stages of revision for publication. The constabulary professionalism of the United Nations peacekeeping force there was subjected to what would be one of its cruelest tests, whatever the final outcome of developments on that strife-rent island.

On July 15, 1974, the Greek Cypriot National Guard, led by Greek mainland officers and abetted by the Athens junta, launched a coup against the government of President Makarios. A staunch enosist, Nikos Sampson, was sworn in as president. Makarios narrowly escaped with his life and managed to flee abroad. Charging that the Greek-engendered coup was an attempt to bring about enosis and thereby threaten the security of the Turkish Cypriot minority, Ankara immediately went on a war footing and deployed warships and landing craft toward Cyprus.

Despite diplomatic talks in London to calm the situation, Turkey would not stay its hand. On July 20, Turkey invaded Cyprus in a dawn seaborne attack on the northern coast backed by paratroop drops near Nicosia. During the invasion day and subsequently, Turkish planes bombed the Nicosia airport and Greek Cypriot garrisons but also inflicted casualties on Cypriot civilians. Athens ordered a full-scale mobilization and sent her navy to sea but never committed her forces to battle. In Cyprus itself, Turkish troops thrust inland amidst heavy initial fighting, but the outgunned and outtrained Cypriot National Guard could not hold the Turkish offensive. Within a few days of the invasion, the Turkish army had firm control over a sizeable beachhead extending from the northern coast town of Kyrenia southward to the Turkish quarter of Nicosia. In subsequent weeks the Turkish invasion force would build up to an estimated 40,000 men.

On July 20, the day of the invasion, United Nations Security Council Resolution 353 called for a halt in the fighting and an end to all foreign military intervention in Cyprus. This included the mainland Greek officers of the Cypriot National Guard as well as the Turkish invasion force. The commander of UNFICYP, Major General Prem Chand, attempted to declare Nicosia an ''open city'' by appealing to Greek and Turkish armed forces to remove themselves from the capital city. But to no avail. UNFICYP observers manning the Green Line in Nicosia were in most cases forced from their positions by the fighting. Secretary-General Waldheim reported to the Security Council that the 2,300-man force of UNFICYP was too small to be effective in light of the postinvasion situation, and requested that the peacekeeping force be increased to 5,000 men.

Heavy fighting continued through July 22, when both Greek and Turkish leaders agreed to a cease-fire under the terms of Security Council Resolution 353. During the latter part of July, however, Turkish forces continued to expand their area of control on Cyprus. On July 23, the military government in Athens resigned, and a civilian government was formed. That same day in Cyprus, Sampson gave up his post and was replaced by the moderate Glefkos Clerides, the president of the House of Representatives. As acting president, Clerides quickly announced his intentions to begin negotiations with Rauf Denktash, the leader of the Cypriot Turkish community and the constitutional vice-president of Cyprus.

On July 25, despite serious violations of the cease-fire, the foreign ministers of Great Britain, Turkey, and Greece—as the original guarantor powers of Cyprus independence—joined in a peace conference at Geneva. The first session of the Geneva conference concluded on July 30 with an agreement by the three foreign ministers to consolidate the cease-fire and to return to Geneva to discuss the island's political future with representatives of the Greek Cypriot and Turkish Cypriot communities. The July

30 agreement of the foreign ministers specifically stipulated that UNFICYP was to demarcate and supervise a buffer zone between the Cypriot National Guard and the Turkish forces, to police Turkish enclaves within Greek-controlled areas, and to insure security in villages of ethnically mixed areas. In recognition of the new power realities, the Geneva confreres acknowledged that the Turkish force would remain on the island until an "acceptable settlement" could be reached.

On August 1, Waldheim noted the provision of the July 30 Geneva agreement. From the standpoint of the UNFICYP role, the major development was that, where the original mandate concerned UNFICYP activities between Greek and Turkish Cypriots, the UN force would now also man a buffer zone between Greek Cypriots and mainland Turkish forces. Waldheim also announced, in what was perceived to be a concession from Ankara, that a "UN presence" would be allowed in Turkish-controlled areas of Cyprus. Nevertheless, less sanguine UN officials in Cyprus reported unofficially that Turkish troops were continuing to pressure UNFICYP out of areas Turkey controlled. In point of fact, UNFICYP units within the Turkish-controlled area were restricted to a few static observation posts with little freedom of movement.

During the first week of August, a multinational military commission, consisting of officers from Great Britain, Turkey, Greece, and UNFICYP, was able to demarcate cease-fire lines from ground maps and helicopter observation. By August 7, UNFICYP strength was up to about 3,750 men, with reinforcement principally coming from Great Britain and Finland, but with Sweden, Canada, Denmark, and Austria also augmenting their contingents. UNFICYP strength would level off at around 4,300 men by the end of 1974.

The second session of the Geneva conference began on August 8 but was overshadowed by continuing fighting in Cyprus. By August 14, the Geneva peace conference collapsed, and a new Turkish offensive started, with planes bombing Nicosia. On August 18, after major Turkish advances, a cease-fire fitfully took hold but not before Turkey had gained control of close to 40 percent of the land area of Cyprus, an area encompassing most of the island's economic wealth. In more starkly human terms, about one-third of the total Greek Cypriot population—fleeing the Turkish invasion—had become refugees. For many of these there would probably never be any going home again. What started out as an effort by enosists to achieve union with Greece by fait accompli ended up with a different fait accompli—a quasi-independent, self-sufficient Turkish part of Cyprus. By the end of 1974, Turkey had already taken initial steps to integrate the Turkish-controlled area of Cyprus with its mainland economy and to colonize areas vacated by refugees with ethnic Turks. Archbishop Makarios's return to Cyprus in early December to resume the presidency added another element to what would be long and contentious negotiations before a Cyprus settlement might be realized. Some sort of cantonal system or biregional federation seemed a probable result.

Whether UNFICYP is destined to play a near-permanent role in Cyprus is a question only the future will answer. But, most likely, any Cypriot accord would involve a United Nations peacekeeping force on the island for a long period. On December 13, 1974, Security Council Resolution 365 endorsed a General Assembly resolution which called upon all parties "to cooperate fully with the United Nations Peacekeeping Force in Cyprus, which may be strengthened if necessary."

When the Cyprus scene exploded, the ineffectiveness of the UN peacekeeping force on the island in controlling the situation made it an object of derision in many quarters. Both Greek and Turkish Cypriot civilians criticized the inability of the United Nations force to prevent detention, looting, displacement of persons, and other violations of human rights. When Cypriot Greek forces attacked several Turkish enclaves, local Turkish leaders accused United Nations units of leaving too precipitously and not returning until well after the cease-fire was in effect. But the major disillusionment was the failure of UNFICYP to extend protection to Greek Cypriot refugees trapped in sectors occupied by the Turkish troops. In the early days of the invasion, large groups of ethnic Greek refugees took haven under the UN flag in the Turkish-surrounded village of Bellapais. For several weeks, despite Turkish harassment, the UN troops were able to protect the besieged refugees and occasionally bring in supplies to them. Eventually, however, Turkish troops unceremoniously pushed the UNFICYP soldiers aside and removed the Greek Cypriot men to points unknown (the women and children were then transported by the UN to Nicosia).

During the peak period of the crisis, peacekeeping for UNFICYP troops often meant pulling each other out of dangerous zones and keeping out of the line of fire. Orders were issued to unit commanders not to fire back even if fired upon but to withdraw from areas of conflict. That the moral authority of the UN force in Cyprus was not entirely negligible, however, was indicated by the fact that the Turkish invasion force did deploy with cognizance of UN positions, few of which were directly over-run in the initial Turkish advances. Turkish pressure to oust UN units typically occurred *after* Turkish control was stabilized. A backhanded indication of the symbolic import of UNFICYP was the frequent tactical decision of Greek Cypriot units to take up positions adjacent to UN outposts, the reasoning being that Turkish attacks would be more hesitant if their fire might hit UN troops. Also important, the moral authority of UNFICYP was accepted by both sides even more so after the UN-supervised cease-fire took hold. It was only under the aegis of UNFICYP that exchange of prisoners of war could take place.

Even though a general order to retreat from combat was given to UNFICYP troops during the peak crisis period, this was not accompanied by an order to withdraw to the safety of main contingent camps. Indeed, UN soldiers in many instances were able to arrange local or temporary cease-fires and deescalate the fighting. No one will ever be able to prove how many lives were thus saved. But many must have been. The fact that the United Nations soldiers were on the scene may also have had an effect on the military conduct of the opposing forces. Without the peace soldiers—surrogate world representatives—looking on, more napalm may have been dropped, more artillery fired on cities, and more atrocities committed.

But above and beyond the humanitarian endeavors and peace-keeping symbolism of UNFICYP, there were those occasions when UN troops were ordered to resist force and did so with remarkable discipline. But not without human cost. In the four months following the outbreak of fighting in Cyprus, nine UNFICYP soldiers were killed and over sixty wounded by hostile fire. Even though operating within the overarching peacekeeping premise of absolute minimal force, the peace soldiers frequently displayed behavior quite in accord with the heroic model of military professionalism.

The most significant display of UNFICYP resistance in the face of overwhelming odds occurred in the United Nations defense of the Nicosia airport. In order to prevent either Greek or Turkish forces from occupying the airport, the UN took control of the facility on July 23. The force commander gave orders to hold the airport even under attack. A UN force consisting of British, Swedes, Canadians, Danes, Austrians, and Finns dug in. A full-scale Turkish assault appeared imminent for a few days but did not materialize. Although official UN reports have made no mention of exchange of fire during the seige of the airport, informal accounts assert UNFICYP troops fired upon Turkish soldiers who attempted to breach the UN perimeter. Whether the Turks really meant to capture the Nicosia airport can be debated, but if they did, they were stopped by the raising of the UN flag and by the determination of the peace soldiers of UNFICYP.

There were also countless other incidents of soldierly valor in the context of the peacekeeping role. One such occurrence was witnessed by millions on network television. Several score guests and employees were pinned down in the lobby of the Ledra Palace Hotel on the Greek side of Nicosia's Green Line. Greek Cypriot national guardsmen in and on the hotel were exchanging fire with Turkish fighters opposite. Two UN soldiers in an UNFICYP jeep—adroitly avoiding the scattered fire of the agitated guardsmen—drove up to the hotel entrance. First beseeching the guardsmen to let them into the hotel, the UN soldiers then succeeded in persuading the guardsmen to a temporary cease-fire, thus permitting the beleaguered occupants to leave. The viewer could not help but marvel at the courage and restraint of the two United Nations soldiers.

Another incident illustrative of the thin line between peacekeeping and martial action took place on July 29, when a

Canadian captain, while escorting a small group of Turkish Cypriot civilians through the Nicosia Green Line, was machine-gunned by Greek Cypriot national guardsmen. As the captain lay wounded in a no-man's-land, other Canadian soldiers, without resorting to fire, tried to effect a rescue. Despite their shouted pleas to the Greek machine-gun crew, the rescuers themselves came under fire. Permission was then asked and received by the Canadians to open fire. UN jeeps with .50 caliber machine guns were brought up, and after a fierce exchange of fire the Greek machine-gun post was knocked out, with at least two Cypriot guardsmen being killed. The Canadians were then able to go forth and recover the severely wounded captain. The Greek commander is reported to have later congratulated the Canadian commander: "You did the right thing. I would have done the same myself."

While the United Nations Force in Cyprus was witness to its own battle casualties, the newly formed United Nations peace-keeping forces in the Middle East were also to suffer losses as they tried to maintain an uneasy truce in the fall of 1974. A Canadian military transport plane on loan to the United Nations was shot down by a missile over Syria with the loss of all nine aboard. Two Austrian UN soldiers were killed when their jeep hit a land mine in the Golan Heights. UN soldiers from Panama, Peru, and Indonesia were killed by Israeli-Egyptian crossfire in the Sinai. It was somberly apparent that peace soldiers were subject to grave risks by interposing themselves between hostile camps whose fury might at any time explode against the men in the middle.

All told, over five hundred UN soldiers have been killed since the inception of international peacekeeping forces. Yet, with the partial exception of the Congo operation, there have been only rare instances in which UN soldiers have shot first. Even more remarkable, there are not too many more instances in which they shot back after receiving fire. As 1974 drew to a close, the ten thousand blue-helmeted soldiers of international peacekeeping forces who were separating Israelis from Arabs in the Middle East, and Greeks from Turks on Cyprus, represented a genuine achievement. If this achievement was not so clearly evident for the efficacy of United Nations peace initiatives, it was certainly so for the manner in which traditional military professionalism could adapt to the novel imperatives of the peace soldier.

Appendix A
Methodology

The information for this study of a United Nations peacekeeping force was based on eight months of full-time field research in Cyprus. Because I had received credentials as an accredited correspondent from the Canadian Defense Ministry and had the cooperation of the United Nations Press Office, I was granted the status of "temporary official assignment" with UNFICYP for the initial two-month period following my arrival in Cyprus in October 1969. This status was regularly renewed until the end of my stay on the island in May 1970. Because of this entree, I was from the beginning allowed virtually complete access to all levels and ranks of UNFICYP. I always went to some lengths to identify myself as a professor with a military sociology specialty; and as time progressed the academic label took precedence over the press identification. During the time of the field research, I spent extended periods with each of the national contingents and was to become a regular loiterer at UNFICYP headquarters. It appears that I was the only individual—excluding United Nations officials—ever to visit all of UNFICYP's constituent units.

In addition to historical, documentary, and autobiographical sources, two systematic sources of primary data were generated in the course of the field research. First, and perhaps most important, I undertook participant observation in a variety of contexts: stationary guard mounts, maneuvers and patrols, investigations of incidents, routine days at headquarters, formal social affairs, stays in the field, and informal nights on the town. During all these occasions, field notes were taken and often shared with UNFICYP confidants. The accounts given in this study on the informal social organization of UNFICYP and the emergence of the constabulary ethic are codifications from these field observations. Over the course of the field research I met and talked with several hundred UNFICYP officers and other ranks. Indeed, inasmuch as the vast majority of the

UNFICYP soldiers rotated back to their home countries on six-month tours, my relatively longer stay led to my becoming a kind of local UNFICYP "old hand" and a repository of much of the lore of the peacekeeping force. UNFICYP military officials would on occasion informally ask me to brief visiting correspondents who were passing through the island.

Second, usually in combination with the field research, I formally interviewed 110 officers—very close to one-third of the entire UNFICYP officer complement. These interviews formed the basis for the tabular data on peacekeeping attitudes presented in the text. An effort was made to interview the officers as late as practicable during their UNFICYP tour, a goal which was in the main achieved; ninety-three of the interviews taking place after the respondent had been on the island over four months. Additionally, from among the 110 interviewees, 25 were subjected to panel interviewing. That is, each of the panel respondents was interviewed three times; during the beginning, middle, and end of their UNFICYP assignments. Specifically, the panel interviews were conducted within the first month of the officer's arrival on Cyprus, the third or fourth month of the tour, and during the final month of UNFICYP duty (most often during the final two weeks).

All interviews were conducted in English, the official language of UNFICYP and the lingua franca of Cyprus. Besides the native English-speakers of the Atlantic contingents, I estimated that close to four-fifths of the officers of Dancon and Swedcon and all of the officers of the Austrian field hospital had adequate or better command of the English language. (Nevertheless, while spending time in a Nordic unit, I was more than once drafted to prepare reports in what was thought to be more polished English.) Only in Fincon was lack of English a problem, where—again estimating—about a quarter of the officers had facility with the language. Of course, regardless of nationality, all headquarters staff officers spoke and wrote Enlgish well.

The selection of the officers to be interviewed was largely determined by convenience and availability—and my own flagging energies. But within these constraints there was a conscious effort to select interviewees proportionate to the ratio of national representation in UNFICYP. Generally speaking, the nationalities of the interviewees were commensurate with overall UNFICYP proportions (excepting the underrepresented Finns). A summary of the UNFICYP officer sample by nationality is as follows:

Nationality	Percentage of UNFICYP (January 1970)	Percentage of Total Interviewed
Austria	4	6
Great Britain	20	23
Canada	13	14
Denmark	20	19
Finland	15	9
Ireland	13	16
Sweden	15	13
Total	100	100
(N)	(334)	(110)

Appendix B
Interview Guide
for UNFICYP
Officer Study

A. Background Information

1. Nationality
2. Unit assignment in UNFICYP
3. Military rank
4. Regular or reserve officer
5. Length of present tour in UNFICYP
6. Prior United Nations peacekeeping service

B. Attitude Items and Code Key

7. We have talked a little about the categories of officer—the manager type, the hero type, the technical type. Could you classify yourself as belonging more or less to one of these types?

a. not coded

8. Does an officer who is well trained in military skills and who has broad leadership experience in his home army still require additional skills for peacekeeping service?

a. yes (constabulary)

b. no (nonconstabulary)

9. Can a soldier be effective in the peacekeeping job if he cannot use force except in self-defense?

a. yes (constabulary)

b. no (nonconstabulary)

10. How would you compare the soldierly qualities of the various national contingents here in UNFICYP?

a. not coded

11. How would you compare the peacekeeping qualities of the various national contingents here in UNFICYP?

a. not coded

12. If it were possible, would you like to make a permanent military career out of UN peacekeeping?

a. yes, definitely

b. yes, with conditions

c. no

13. Do you think UN assignment helps or hurts your military career at home, or does it make any difference?

a. helps career

b. no difference

c. hurts career

14. Has serving with UNFICYP changed any of your ideas about the need for a stronger United Nations or perhaps even a form of world government?

a. more internationalist

b. no change

c. less internationalist

15. In the imaginary situation where there would be a conflict between your home country and the United Nations, with which side would you probably be in sympathy?

a. United Nations

b. indeterminate

c. home country

16. Why do you think your country decided to take part in UNFICYP?

a. idealistic or altruistic motives

b. mixed motives

c. national self-interest or cynical motives

17. What do you think is the general attitude of the civilian population in your country toward the army and military life in general?

a. favorable

b. mixed

c. unfavorable

18. Do you think there have been major changes in the social life and morals of your country in recent years? If so, do you think these changes have been for the better or worse, or does it make any difference to you?

a. for better

b. no difference

c. for worse

19. On political matters at home, with whom would you say you generally agree—the left, the right, or the center?

a. left

b. center

c. right

20. Generally speaking, how successful an operation has UNFICYP been?
a. largely successful
b. partly successful
c. failure

21. You have probably heard it said that peacekeeping is not a soldier's job, but only a soldier can do it. What do you think of that?
a. not coded

Notes

Portions of the narrative in the chapters dealing with the history of peacekeeping and the formation of UNFICYP rely heavily upon and paraphrase the discussions found in Larry L. Fabian, *Soldiers without Enemies* (Washington, D. C.: Brookings Institution, 1971); R. J. Hill, *Command and Control Problems of UN and Similar Peacekeeping Forces*, ORD Report no. 68/R5 (Ottawa, Canada: Department of National Defense, 1968); James A. Stegenga, *The United Nations Force in Cyprus* (Columbus: Ohio State University Press, 1968); and David Wainhouse et al., *International Peace Observation* (Baltimore: Johns Hopkins Press, 1968).

Chapter 1

1. The concept of the constabulary model of armed forces was first introduced by Morris Janowitz, *The Professional Soldier* (Glencoe, Ill.: Free Press, 1960), pp. 418–41. For more recent statements by Janowitz on the constabulary model see his "Armed Forces and Society," in Jacques van Doorn, ed., *Armed Forces and Society* (The Hague: Mouton, 1968), pp. 15–38; and "Toward a Redefinition of Military Strategy in International Relations," *World Politics* 26 (July 1974): 471–508.

2. Although UNITAR has been advised by the UN Secretariat to avoid research or training on peacekeeping operations per se, it did cosponsor with the International Peace Academy a 1973 conference on the more vague topic of "Settlement of Disputes under United Nations Auspices." Marlyse Messing, "UNITAR Studies on Peaceful Settlement," *UNITAR News* 5, no. 1 (1973): 22–24.

3. Indar Jit Rikhye, "Preparation and Training of United Nations Peacekeeping Forces," *Adelphi Paper No. 9* (London: Institute for

Strategic Studies, 1963); and idem, *United Nations Peace-Keeping Operations—Higher Conduct*, IPKO Monograph no. 1 (Paris: International Information Center on Peace-Keeping Operations, 1967).

4. Reviews of the peacekeeping literature are found in Albert Legault, *Peace-Keeping Operations: Bibliography* (Paris: International Information Center on Peace-Keeping Operations, 1967); Malvern Lumsden, "Research on International Peace-Keeping Forces: A Scanning of Institutions," *Journal of Peace Research*, no. 2 (1966): 194–96; and James A. Stegenga, "Peacekeeping: Postmortems or Previews," *International Organization* 27 (Summer 1973): 373–85.

5. A representative selection of major studies on peacekeeping issues is: Lincoln P. Bloomfield, *International Military Forces* (Boston: Little, Brown, 1964), revised as Bloomfield, *The Power to Keep Peace* (Berkeley, Calif.: World Without War Council, 1971); D. W. Bowett et al., *United Nations Forces* (New York: Praeger, 1964); Arthur L. Burns and Nina Heathcote, *Peace-Keeping by U.N. Forces* (New York: Praeger, 1963); Jack Citrin, *United Nations Peacekeeping Activities* (Denver: University of Denver, 1965); Granville Clark and Louis B. Sohn, *World Peace Through World Law* (Cambridge, Mass.: Harvard University Press, 1962); Inis L. Claude, Jr., "United Nations Use of Military Force," *Journal of Conflict Resolution* 7 (1963): 117–29; Fabian, *Soldiers Without Enemies;* Rosalyn Higgins, *United Nations Peacekeeping*, vol. 1, *The Middle East* (London: Oxford University Press, 1969), vol. 2, *Asia* (London: Oxford University Press, 1970); Alan James, *The Politics of Peace-Keeping* (New York: Praeger, 1969); Evan Luard, "United Nations Peace Forces," in Luard, ed., *The Evolution of International Organizations* (New York: Praeger, 1966), pp. 138–76; Lester B. Pearson, "Force for the U.N.," *Foreign Affairs* 35 (April 1957): 395–404; Ruth B. Russell, *United Nations Experience with Military Force* (Washington, D.C.: Brookings Institution, 1965); Indar Jit Rikhye et al., *The Thin Blue Line* (New Haven, Conn.: Yale University Press, 1975); Finn Seyersted, *United Nations Forces in the Law of Peace and War* (Leyden: A. W. Sijthoff, 1966); Brian E. Urquhart, "United Nations Peace Forces and the Changing United Nations," *International Organization* 17 (Spring 1963): 338–54; Wainhouse et al., *International Peace Observation;* idem, *International Peacekeeping at the Crossroads* (Baltimore: Johns Hopkins University Press, 1973); and Walter L. Williams, Jr., *Intergovernmental Military Forces and World Public Order* (Dobbs Ferry, N.Y.: Oceana, 1971).

6. See, for example, Bloomfield, *The Power to Keep Peace;* Bowett et al., *United Nations Forces;* Clark and Sohn, *World Peace Through World Law;* Arthur M. Cox, *Prospects for Peacekeeping* (Washington, D.C.: Brookings Institution, 1967); William R. Frye, *A United Nations Peace*

Force (New York: Oceana, 1957); Per Frydenberg, ed., *Peace-Keeping Experience and Evaluation* (Oslo: Norwegian Institute of International Affairs, 1964); and UNA-USA, *Controlling Conflicts in the 1970s* (New York: United Nations Association of the United States of America, 1969).

7. Gabriella Rosner, *The United Nations Emergency Force* (New York: Columbia University Press, 1963); Ernest W. Lefever, *United Nations Peacekeeping in the Congo* (Washington, D.C.: Brookings Institution, 1966); and Stegenga, *The United Nations Force in Cyprus*.

8. James M. Boyd, *United Nations Peace-Keeping Operations* (New York: Praeger, 1971); E. L. M. Burns, *Between Arab and Israeli* (Toronto: Clark and Irwin, 1962); Michael Harbottle, *The Impartial Soldier* (London: Oxford University Press, 1970); Hill, *Command and Control Problems*; L. M. K. Stern, *Military Staffing at UN Headquarters for Peace-Keeping Operations*, IPKO Monograph no. 3 (Paris: International Information Center on Peace-Keeping Operations, 1967); Carl von Horn, *Soldiering for Peace* (New York: David McKay, 1966); and A. J. Wilson, *Some Principles for Peace-Keeping Operations*, IPKO Monograph no. 2 (Paris: International Information Center on Peace-Keeping Operations, 1967). The writings of Burns, Hill, and von Horn are noteworthy in that they reflect a military perspective critical of United Nations civilian officials. A military viewpoint more sympathetic with the UN organization is found in Indar Jit Rikhye, Michael Harbottle, and Bjøorn Egge, *The Thin Blue Line* (New Haven: Yale University Press, 1974).

9. Although some references may have escaped my attention, studies directly applicable to the military sociology of international peacekeeping force seem limited to the following: Henry V. Dicks, "National Loyalty, Identity, and the International Soldier," in Bloomfield, *The Power to Keep Peace*, pp. 133–51; J. A. Jackson, "The Irish Army and the Development of the Constabulary Concept," in van Doorn, *Armed Forces and Society*, pp. 109–26; Johan Galtung, "U.N. Forces and Non-Violence" (in Norwegian), *Pax*, no. 8 (1963), cited in Hanna Newcombe and Alan Newcombe, *Peace Research Around the World* (Oakville, Ontario: Canadian Peace Research Institute, 1969), p. 175; Jan H. Mans, "United Nations Forces: The Strain between Proposal and Reality" (in Dutch), *Internationale Spectator* 24 (November 1970): 1749–73; David N. Solomon, "The Soldierly Self and the Peace-Keeping Role: Canadian Officers in Peace-Keeping Forces," in van Doorn, *Military Profession and Military Regimes*, pp. 52–69; Jacques van Doorn and Jan H. Mans, "United Nations Forces: On Legitimacy and Effectiveness of International Military Operations," in van Doorn, *Armed Forces*

and Society, pp. 345–76; and Steinar Witgil, "Neutrality and Partisanship of the Impartial Soldier," paper presented at the Seventh World Congress of Sociology, Varna, Bulgaria, 1970. From the above citations, only the studies of Solomon and Witgil report data obtained from United Nations soldiers, and these limited to soldiers from one nationality in post-peacekeeping interviews.

Deserving special comment is the work of Verner Goldschmidt, who has spent extended periods with the Danish contingent of the United Nations Force in Cyprus. Through his field research, Goldschmidt has sought to specify how a peacekeeping force can operate as a mediating agency between hostile communities. See Verner Goldschmidt, *Konflikt Uden Vold* [Conflict without violence] (Copenhagen: Glydendalske Boghandel, 1974). It is to be hoped that this important study will soon be translated into non-Danish languages, thus allowing for a wider readership. For another intriguing formulation of peacekeeping, ranging from United Nations forces to family crises, see Karl L. Schonborn, *Dealing with Violence* (Springfield, Ill.: Charles Thomas, 1974).

10. Van Doorn and Mans, "United Nations Forces."

Chapter 2

1. Inis L. Claude, Jr., "The Peace-Keeping Role of the United Nations," in E. Berkeley Tompkins, ed., *The United Nations in Perspective* (Stanford, Calif.: Hoover Institution Press, 1972), p. 52. Another insightful overview of United Nations peacekeeping is A. J. R. Groom, "Peacekeeping: Perspectives and Progress," *International Affairs* 47 (April 1971): 340–52.

2. Although regional peacekeeping forces are not included in the purview of the present study, special mention can be made of two such instances. In 1964, Nigerian and Ethiopian military units were sent to Tanzania upon that government's request to the Organization of African Unity. The Nigerian-Ethiopian contingents replaced the British, who had initially been called by President Nyerere to restore order following a mutiny in the Tanzania army. In 1969, following the outbreak of hostilities between El Salvador and Honduras, the Organization of American States was requested by the disputants to send a truce-supervising force. In neither the OAU nor the OAS peacekeeping operations, however, did the constituent military units serve under a central command.

3. J. Brind, "League of Nations: Report by the Commander in Chief, International Force in the Saar, 26 October, 1935," *IPKO Documenta-*

tion No. 29 (Paris: International Information Center on Peace-Keeping Operations, 1968).

4. A listing of the more important of these United Nations peace-keeping missions follows: United Nations Commission for Indonesia (UNCI), 1947–51; United Nations Truce Supervision Organization (UNTSO), variously in Palestine, Israel, and Suez sector, 1948–present; United Nations Commission for India and Pakistan (UNCIP), 1948–49, later the United Nations Military Observer Group in India and Pakistan (UNMOGIP) in Kashmir, 1949–present; United Nations Observer Group in Lebanon (UNOGIL), 1958; United Nations Temporary Executive Authority (UNTEA) and United Nations Security Force (UNSF) in West New Guinea (Western Irian), 1962–63; United Nations Yemen Observation Mission (UNYOM), 1962–64; and United Nations India-Pakistan Observation Mission (UNIPOM), 1965–66. Not included as bona-fide peacekeeping operations are those United Nations missions whose impartiality was open to question owing to a too close association with the Western position in Cold War confrontations: United Nations Special Committee on the Balkans (UNSCOB), 1947–54 in Greece; and the United Nations Commission on Korea (UNCOK), 1948–50.

An informative account of the military observer in UN peacekeeping missions is Erling Lund, "Observation Service," in Frydenberg, *Peace-Keeping Experience and Evaluation*, pp. 147–61.

5. Fabian, *Soldiers Without Enemies*, p. 67. It is also germane to note that the expressions "United Nations Military Force" or "United Nations Armed Forces" have been studiously avoided in the designations of all UN peacekeeping forces.

6. Readable and informative accounts of the conflicts within the United Nations force in the Congo from the personal vantage points of key participants are: Connor Cruise O'Brien, *To Katanga and Back: A UN Case History* (New York: Grosset and Dunlap, 1962); and von Horn, *Soldiering For Peace*, pp. 140–252.

7. UN Document, S/4741, 21 February 1961.

8. UN Document, S/5575, 4 March 1963.

9. During the early stages of the Cyprus peacekeeping operation, the Czechoslovakian government offered to contribute a military unit to the United Nations force. But American and British pressure prevailed upon U Thant not to accept the offer. Earlier Czechoslovakia and Rumania had volunteered military units to the first United Nations Emergency Force in the Middle East, but again Western pressures precluded the Secretariat from accepting socialist bloc contingents. Cox, *Prospects for Peace-keeping*, p. 43.

10. UN Document, A/3943, 9 October 1958.

11. Lester Pearson's peacekeeping proposals are cited and discussed in Fabian, *Soldiers Without Enemies*, pp. 82–83.

12. U Thant, "United Nations Peace Force," an address to the Harvard Alumni Association delivered June 13, 1963. UN Press Release SG/1520, 12 June 1963.

13. Starting with Dag Hammarskjöld and continuing with his successors, the secretary-general and his staff have become the executors of peacekeeping arrangements. Legally speaking, the secretary-general's executive management of UN peacekeeping operations derives from Article 97 of the Charter which charges the secretary-general with being the "chief administrative officer of the Organization." But in specific peacekeeping forces, such authority also derives from the authorizing resolutions of the Security Council or General Assembly. In pursuance of the execution of enabling United Nations resolutions, several levels of peacekeeping accords must be negotiated by the Secretariat.

First, there must be a "Status of Forces" agreement with the host country. The significant precedent was established in 1956 with the first UNEF, in an exchange of letters between the secretary-general and the Egyptian government in which explicit terms were set forth on the legal status and privileges of the UN forces, including areas of criminal and civil jurisdiction. Similar status-of-forces agreements were worked out in ONUC, UNFICYP, the second UNEF, and UNDOF. Second, there are "Participating Agreements" between the Secretariat and those states which place their contingents at the disposal of the United Nations. Legal bonds, that is, have to be forged between the United Nations and states participating in peacekeeping operations through a network of bilateral arrangements. Third are the "General Regulations" which specify the command and control guidelines under which the peacekeeping force must operate. Here the subject is delimiting lines of responsibility between the secretary-general, other UN civilian officials, the force commander, and the national contingents. Finally, there are the "Standing Operating Procedures" which are developed by the force commander in consultation with the Secretariat. Such "S.O.P.'s" specify how the peacekeeping force conducts itself on a day-to-day basis, e.g. restrictions on force, nature and frequency of reports, areas of responsibility within the military command, dress and discipline of troops, and so on.

14. Since its admission to the United Nations in 1971, China has not participated in any votes in the Security Council on peacekeeping forces. Symbolically, nonparticipation in a Security Council vote falls between a

veto and an abstention. This choice of action reflects China's opposition
to the intervention principle implicit in the deployment of peacekeeping
forces.

Chapter 3

1. Stegenga, *The United Nations Force in Cyprus*, p. 19.
2. Ibid., pp. 66–67.
3. UN Document, S/5575, 4 March 1964, par. 4–6.
4. An evaluation of the intricate and sometimes purposely obscured
financial arrangements between the Secretariat, UNFICYP, members of
the United Nations, and nations contributing troops to UNFICYP is
beyond the competence of this writer. However, the following summary
statement may shed some illumination on the topic. "But the Scandinavian nations providing volunteer mercenary units insisted that the
United Nations reimburse them for nearly all the costs incurred (pay, per
diem and overseas allowances, and so forth), whereas Britain and Canada
each paid all the costs of supporting their units. Only Ireland among
those countries providing major volunteer mercenary units paid the costs
of supporting its contingent, and then only for the first year" (Stegenga,
United Nations Force in Cyprus, p. 88).
5. UNCIVPOL had precedents of a sort in the internationally recruited
civilian police used by the League of Nations for duty in the Saar
International Force. There was also the use of Nigerian civil policemen in
ONUC, and UNTEA in West New Guinea had the local Papuan police at
its disposal. Nevertheless, only in UNFICYP were civilian policemen to
play an important role in a peacekeeping operation. The multinational
UNCIVPOL is worthy of a study in its own right.
6. UN Document, S/7350, 10 June 1966, para. 29.

Chapter 4

1. UN Document, S/5653, 11 April 1964.
2. Stegenga, *The United Nations Force in Cyprus*, pp. 10–11.
3. For accounts of the ways in which a UN force commander can come
into conflict with high-level UN civilian staff, see Hill, *Command and
Control Problems*, especially pp. 20 and 26; von Horn, *Soldiering for
Peace*, especially pp. 199–203, 222–23, 254–56, and 308–12.
4. The principal UNFICYP liaison officer for the Greek Cypriots was
Irish; for the Turkish Cypriots the officer was a Finn. These national
choices for liaison officers—perhaps reaching a little too far for putative

commonalities—were allegedly determined on the presumption that a representative from Ireland, with its own partition problems, would be more congenial to the Greek side; while the Finns and Turks shared a mutual Altaic linguistic origin.

5. The absence of a formal intelligence section in United Nations peacekeeping forces has always been troublesome for military commanders. See Hill, *Command and Control Problems*, p. 28. Noteworthy is that the absence of an intelligence section was also a point of contention on the part of the commander of the League of Nations International Force in the Saar. Wainhouse et al, *International Peace Observation*, p. 27.

6. In 1970, the UNFICYP military police company consisted of five officers (two each from Canada and Denmark, and one from Sweden) and 60 other ranks: Great Britain 8, Canada 15, Denmark 17, Finland 7, Ireland 4, and Sweden 9.

7. The maximum detention punishment within UNFICYP ranged from ninety days in Cancon to fifteen in Swedcon; maximum fines ranged from 60 percent of one-month's pay in Cancon to no fines in Fincon. Generally speaking, more severe punishments could be meted out to the regular soldiers of the Atlantic contingents compared to the reservists of the Nordic contingents.

8. Over the course of the ten years following UNFICYP's formation there have been two public scandals involving violation of the canon of impartiality by UNFICYP soldiers. In both cases there was the selling of arms to Turkish Cypriots: in the one by British soldiers and in the other by Swedes. In the British case monetary gain was the obvious motive, while for the Swedish malefactors political sympathies for the Turkish cause seem to have played a part. Both cases occurred early in UNFICYP's existence, and the culprits were subjected to severe court-martial penalties.

9. It must be noted that French-speaking Canadian contingents have also been regularly assigned to UNFICYP. But the general statement on English-language facility applies here too.

10. My estimated proportions of those having adequate English command in the non-Atlantic contingents of UNFICYP are:

	Officers	Other Ranks
Dancon	80%	40%
Fincon	25%	10%
Swedcon	80%	50%
Austrian hospital	100%	30%

11. Successfully endeavoring to come up with photographs of other than United Nations soldiers, the intrepid *Blue Beret* photographer initiated a "Miss UNFICYP" series of comely women. That the photographer could come up with a new "Miss UNFICYP" every week bespoke extraordinary diligence in tracking down field service secretaries, wives or daughters of UNFICYP officers, and occasional tourists.

12. A formulation of the conditions supportive of a peacekeeping force with regard to the local population has been offered in Ingrid Galtung and Johan Galtung, "Some Factors Affecting Local Acceptance of the UN Force: A Pilot Project Report from Gaza," *International Problems* (Israel), nos. 1–2 (1966), cited and summarized in Legault, *Peace-Keeping Operations: Bibliography*, pp. 48–49. The authors present their arguments *a contrario*, listing the following traits as ones that should not characterize a peacekeeping force: (1) display of conspicuous consumption; (2) a stay defined as permanent or open-ended; (3) composition consisting of one nation only, and an unpopular one; (4) no engagement in good deeds; (5) no contact with population, or highly unpopular fraternization; (6) no symbols of internationalism; (7) conspicuous demonstration of power; (8) suppression of political activity; (9) highly efficient direction of the civilian population; and (10) diffused military role of the peacekeeping force.
Yet UNFICYP was readily accepted by both Greek and Turkish Cypriots even though it departed from many of the criteria enumerated by the Galtungs. Thus: (1) the purchases of goods and services from the local economy by UNFICYP soldiers at high levels of consumption was recognized to the extent that the force was referred to as "Cyprus's favorite tourists"; (2) UNFICYP's stay was open-ended and semi-permanent; (3) UNFICYP's major military component was from Great Britain, a country whose military forces had been the object of Greek Cypriot guerilla warfare only a few years earlier; (4) there was virtually no personal contact between UNFICYP soldiers and the local population; and (5) the UNFICYP military role was notably diffuse in manifold economic normalization activities.

13. A survey of Cypriot secondary school students found Greek Cypriots preferring UN forces that were perceived as coming from weak nations (Finland, Ireland), while Turkish Cypriots preferred UN forces that were regarded as representative of strong nations (Great Britain, Sweden). Malvern Lumsden, "Some Factors Affecting Local Acceptance of a UN Force," in Bengt Hoglund and Jorgen W. Ulrich, eds., *Conflict Control and Conflict Resolution* (Copenhagen: Munksgaard, 1974), in press.

14. Ralph Allen, "Fourteen Days in Cyprus," *Maclean's* 57 (June 20,

1964): 40, as quoted in Stegenga, *United Nations Force in Cyprus*, p. 148.

Chapter 5

1. A study reflecting Canadian military viewpoints concludes that all United Nations forces "have been successful when they enforce their own rights, and proved worthless whenever they have let local forces treat them with contempt" (Hill, *Command and Control Problems*, p. 25). The commander of the first UNEF has argued that a peacekeeping force must "have a full, sustained combat capability" (E. L. M. Burns, "The Withdrawal of UNEF and the Future of Peace-Keeping," *International Journal*, 23 [Winter 1967-68]: 167-97). General Carl von Horn, in discussing his efforts to persuade the United Nations civilian staff of the need for military preparedness in the ONUC force, writes: "At any rate, the proposal made extremely sound sense and would have been unhesitatingly adopted in any normal army. Unfortunately we were not 'any army'; we were a United Nations Force in which logic, military principles—even common sense—took second place to political factors" (*Soldiering for Peace*, pp. 158-59).

2. Hill, *Command and Control Problems*, pp. 22-23, notes how ONUC was characterized by conflicting commands. "The UN's continued failure to authorize moves to end Katangan secession . . . led to virtual indiscipline among UN officers during the further trial of strength which occurred in December 1962. UN troops . . . pushed on . . . despite an order from the Secretary-General to halt. . . . Success brought approval, but in less fortunate circumstances similar indiscipline could have resulted in disaster."

3. On the issue of the relations of national military establishments with United Nations forces, it is germane that informed observers have noted that, whereas in Nordic countries the defense ministries most consistently advocate peacekeeping participation and the foreign ministries try to hold back, in Canada this is not so clear and may be the reverse. Wainhouse et al., *International Peacekeeping at the Crossroads*, p. 371.

4. Harbottle, *The Impartial Soldier*, p. 109.

5. The relatively low remuneration for British participants in UNFICYP vs. the Nordic contingents had a historical parallel in the League of Nations International Force in the Saar. British soldiers in the League force received a per diem allowance of twelve and a half francs daily compared to thirty-three francs for members of the Swedish contingent. Wainhouse et al., *International Peace Observation*, p. 28.

6. For other commentaries on the friction between civilian and military

members within UN peacekeeping operations, see Hill, *Command and Control Problems*, pp. 9, 15; von Horn, *Soldiering for Peace*, pp. 170–80, 252–62; Rosner, *The United Nations Emergency Force*, pp. 136–37; and Lund, "Observation Service," in Frydenberg, *Peace-Keeping Experience and Evaluation*, pp. 147–61.

7. Samuel P. Huntington, *The Soldier and the State* (New York: Vintage, 1964), pp. 80–85.

Chapter 6

1. In discussion of authority in standard military forces, the distinction has been made between "leadership" and "command." Where the former arises out of personal qualities in the combat or field situation in the front echelon, the latter derives from rational ends-means calculation and predominates in the rear echelon. Maury D. Feld, "Information and Authority: The Structure of Military Organization," *American Sociological Review* 24 (February 1959): 15–22. While there is an inherent antinomy between the two forms of authority in standard armed forces, peacekeeping forces can be conceived of as almost entirely a command organization.

2. UN Document, S/5653, 11 April 1964.

3. A good insider's account of how the threat—but not employment— of force by UNFICYP resolved one intercommunal crisis is given in Michael Harbottle, a former UNFICYP chief of staff, in his *The Impartial Soldier*, pp. 82–91. Greek Cypriot soldiers backed down from threatening a Turkish village in the face of a multinational UNFICYP show of force. Harbottle concludes his assessment of the incident as follows: "There is no doubt that our firm and forceful stand strengthened our prestige and sweetened our image among many who had come to look upon us as a rather ineffective agency for peace."

4. On the importance of peer groups in the information channels of peacekeeping units, see Steinar Witgil, "Neutrality and Partisanship."

5. The fundamentally similar terms in which both Cypriot communities were regarded was humorously illustrated in an informal newsletter distributed to Britcon troops. A Turkish Cypriot was defined as one who drinks Turkish coffee and eats kebabs; a Greek Cypriot as one who drinks Turkish coffee and eats kebabs but calls it something else.

6. A survey of Norwegian soldiers who had served with the first UNEF suggested that partiality on the side of one party might be fostered by not having contact with that party (the Israelis in this case). Witgil, "Neutrality and Partisanship."

Chapter 7

1. On the conservative nature of the professional officer corps in Western parliamentary democracies, see Janowitz, *Professional Soldier*, pp. 233–56; Huntington, *The Soldier and the State*, pp. 59–97; and Bengt Abrahamsson, *Military Professionalization and Political Power* (Beverly Hills, Calif.: Sage, 1972), pp. 101–11.

2. For portrayals of the decline in status of the armed forces in the United States as well as in other Western societies, from the viewpoint of military personnel, see Ward Just, *Military Men* (New York: Alfred Knopf, 1970); Symposium International de Sociologie Militaire, *Les Militaires et leur formation* (Paris: Arpajonaise, 1970); Julio Busquets, *El Militar de Carrera en España* (Barcelona: Ediciones Ariel, 1971); J. C. M. Baynes, *The Soldier in Modern Society* (London: Eyre Methuen, 1972); Edward L. King, *The Death of the Army* (New York: Saturday Review Press, 1972); and George Walton, *The Tarnished Shield* (New York: Dodd, Mead, 1973). From the academic side, it was significant that the theme "The Crisis of Legitimacy" was adopted for the meetings of the Research Committee on Armed Forces and Society, International Sociological Association, Toronto, Canada, 1974.

3. Hayward R. Alker, "The Politics of Supranationalism in the United Nations," paper presented at Peace Research Conference, Chicago, 1964, cited in Hanna Newcombe and Alan Newcombe, *Peace Research Around the World*, pp. 37–38. The terms "internationalism," "transnationalism," and "supranationalism" have acquired a certain interchangeability. From a strictly semantic viewpoint, however, "supranationalism" comes closest to the concept we are referring to in assessing the attitudes of UNFICYP officers toward the United Nations and world bodies. Nevertheless, even at the risk of some loss in conceptual rigor, the term "internationalism" is preferred in this study owing to its common usage.

4. It must be noted that the interview question per se ascertained changes in attitudes toward internationalism rather than absolute attitudes toward internationalism. It is conceivable, for example, that an officer who shifted from a one-world position to preference for a strong United Nations would be classified as "less internationalist" in the coding; while a person who changed from a staunch nationalist to one with a preference for a weak United Nations would be coded "more internationalist." The incidence of such responses among the interviewed UNFICYP officers, however, was rare if at all. We are fairly confident that the perceived changes in internationalism correlated almost perfectly with absolute levels of internationalist identification.

5. Although the table presented in the text runs internationalist

attitudes by constabulary ethic, there is no temporal or logical priority for either of the two variables. Accordingly, the same data is presented below but with constabulary ethic by internationalist attitudes. If anything, the low order of correlation between the two variables becomes even more evident.

	Constabulary	Non-constabulary	Total	(N)
More internationalist	60	40	100%	(25)
No change	48	52	100%	(43)
Less internationalist	50	50	100%	(42)

Chapter 8

1. A participant in the United Nations force in the Congo has similarly observed that when the peacekeeping soldiers first arrived they displayed a sense of being champions of a United Nations cause; but that the ideal of internationalism faded noticeably over the course of the peacekeeping tour. Gustav C. Bowitz, "Central Administration of U.N. Security Forces," in Frydenberg, *Peace-Keeping Experience and Evaluation*, p. 107.

2. There has been considerable discussion of analytic induction in the sociological literature. See, particularly, Ralph H. Turner, "The Quest for Universals in Sociological Research," *American Sociological Review* 18 (December 1953): 604–11. For studies which have used the analytic induction method, see Alfred R. Lindesmith, *Opiate Addiction* (Bloomington, Ind.: Principia Press, 1947); Donald R. Cressey, *Other People's Money* (Glencoe, Ill.: Free Press, 1953); Howard S. Becker, *Outsiders* (New York: Free Press of Glencoe, 1963); and John Lofland, *Doomsday Cult* (Englewood Cliffs, N. J.: Prentice-Hall, 1966). The phraseology of the analytic induction method given here relies heavily on Lofland, *Doomsday Cult*, pp. 31–34.

Chapter 9

1. A study of the retrospective attitudes of Canadian military officers with peacekeeping experience is consistent with the proposition that the constabulary ethic derives primarily from learning experiences in the field rather than from prior peacekeeping training or socialization. David N.

Solomon, "The Soldierly Self and the Peace-Keeping Role," in Jacques van Doorn, ed., *Military Profession and Military Regimes* (The Hague: Mouton, 1969), pp. 52–68.

2. It is also the case that the first peacekeeping force—the International Force in the Saar of the League of Nations—was an unqualified success even though not "peace trained" in any sense. Wainhouse et al., *International Peace Observation*, pp. 25–29.

3. A leading researcher on international organizations has found that, over the course of participation in the United Nations, delegates became less parochial and more aware and sensitive to the positions of other national representatives. Participation in the United Nations, that is, led to a general broadening experience in which the delegates increasingly saw other national interests in varying shades of gray and less in blacks and whites. This can be interpreted as evidence that participation in United Nations activities increases internationalist attitudes. See Chadwick F. Alger, "United Nations Participation as a Learning Experience," *Public Opinion Quarterly* 27 (Fall 1963): 411–26; and Alger, "Personal Contact in Intergovernmental Organizations," in Herbert C. Kelman, ed., *International Behavior* (New York: Holt, Rinehart, Winston, 1965), pp. 523–47.

Although the Alger data might seem at odds with the UNFICYP evidence, where United Nations assignment did not increase the internationalism of serving officers, the inconsistency may be more apparent than real. For the Alger findings specifically demonstrated a rise in transnationalism (greater tolerance across national lines) and did not directly measure supranationalism (adherence to the United Nations). The UNFICYP findings, it is to be stressed, referred to increasing skepticism toward the United Nations as a world body rather than to any heightened chauvinism toward other national contingents. Indeed, it seemed that the UNFICYP officers became more transnational while becoming less supranational. Or to use a Freudian metaphor, the relationships of the national contingents toward the United Nations and each other were more Oedipal than they were cases of sibling rivalry.

4. On the issue of the lack of glorification of war among military professionals, see Janowitz, *Professional Soldier*, pp. 215–32; and Huntington, *The Soldier and the State*, pp. 68–70.

5. An excellent statement on the theoretical development of the concept of military professionalism is Arthur D. Larson, "Military Professionalism and Civil Control," *Journal of Political and Military Sociology* 2 (Spring 1974): 57–72.

6. Janowitz, *Professional Soldier*, pp. 38–53.

Index